THE

Insider's
GUIDE
TO
Medical School
ADMISSIONS

By
Rolando Stephen Toyos, M.D.

THE

Insider's
GUIDE
TO
Medical School
ADMISSIONS

By
Rolando Stephen Toyos, M.D.

CAREER PRESS
3 Tice Road
P.O. Box 687
Franklin Lakes, NJ 07417
1-800-CAREER-1
201-848-0310 (NJ and outside U.S.)
FAX: 201-848-1727

THE INSIDER'S GUIDE TO MEDICAL SCHOOL ADMISSIONS
ISBN 1-56414-272-8, $16.99
Cover design by Tom Phon
Printed in the U.S.A. by Book-mart Press

To order this title by mail, please include price as noted above, $2.50 handling per order, and $1.50 for each book ordered. Send to: Career Press, Inc., 3 Tice Road, P.O. Box 687, Franklin Lakes, NJ 07417.

Or call toll-free 1-800-CAREER-1 (NJ and Canada: 201-848-0310) to order using VISA or MasterCard, or for further information on books from Career Press.

Library of Congress Cataloging-in-Publication Data

Toyos, Rolando Stephen, 1966-
    The insider's guide to medical school admissions / by Rolando
Stephen Toyos.
        p.   cm.
    Includes index.
    ISBN 1-56414-272-8 (pbk.)
        1. Medical colleges--United States--Admission--Handbooks, manuals,
etc. 2. Medicine--Vocational guidance--Handbooks, manuals, etc.
3. Medical education--United States--Handbooks, manuals, etc.
I. Title.
R838.4.T68 1997
610'.71'173--dc21   96-37945
                                                                   CIP

OCT 28 1997

Acknowledgments ⎯⎯⎯⎯⎯⎯⎯⎯⎯⎯ /\\

I would like to express my appreciation to the many people who directly or indirectly helped with this book including: Dr. Peter Rodgers, Dr. William Wallce, Dr. David Toovy, Dr. Tim Ruark, Charlene Pyskoty, the Myintoo family, medical and premedical students at the University of Illinois, Harvard University, University of California at San Francisco, Chicago Medical School, University of Southern California, and Stanford University.

Contributing author, Troy Foster
Second year medical student, Northwestern University Medical School.

Contents _____

Foreword ⎯⎯⎯⎯⎯⎯⎯⎯⎯⎯⎯⎯⎯⎯⎯⎯

I was honored when Dr. Rolando Stephen Toyos asked me to write the foreword of his book on gaining admission and succeeding in medical school. Medical school has experienced incredible changes in the last few years. The emphasis on what medical schools are looking for in applicants has changed. Gone are the days when students are selected based only on their command of undergraduate science courses. Schools are looking for multidimensional students who not only can handle their science courses but are equipped with keen interpersonal skills. Because schools are requiring more of their applicants, the process of applying for admission has become more complex. Dr. Toyos's book provides the student with a step-by-step approach to gain acceptance into medical school. I believe as a bonus the book offers many strategies on how to select a school, receive financial aid, gain acceptance after being rejected, and achieve maximum performance once in medical school.

I have known Dr. Toyos since the day I interviewed him as an applicant to the University of Illinois College of Medicine. His application and interview were stellar. At that time, I was impressed with his undergraduate and graduate career at University of California, Berkeley and Stanford University, respectively. He was also a decorated high school science teacher and counselor. He used his experiences to excel in medical school in many ways including academics, school government, research, tutoring, and third- and fourth-year clerkships. Upon graduating medical school, he won the school's Merck Award for Academic Achievement. He is now completing a residency in Ophthalmology at Northwestern University, but still continues to successfully assist premedical and medical students. I believe there is no better person to teach the prospective student how to gain admission and achieve his or her highest potential in medical school.

Dr. William Wallace
Dean of Student Affairs
University of Illinois College of Medicine

Preface

The Insider's Guide to Medical School Admissions offers a unique perspective on gaining admission to and succeeding in medical school. I have gone through the process as a student and also as a teacher, advisor, and school representative. I have had the opportunity to see the process from the school's and student's point of view. The strategies in this book have been used successfully by high school, premedical, and medical students.

I decided to create a workbook type format because during the process you will be using the book as a reference and also adding your own notes. You will also be able to use the book as a way to organize your admission applications and information gathered from the schools.

The book will help you during all four years in medical school with advice on how to study, examination tips, a recommended booklist, and practical information about your clinical years.

Finally, I was very pleased with the response I received from the first version of this book. While talking to premedical and medical students about the book, they gave me suggestions on how to make the book even better. This new edition keeps the original format of premedical and medical school strategies for success while adding more sections like an MCAT preparatory section, added information on each medical school, and a National Boards study guide for use in clerkships and also in test preparation.

You have chosen a career that requires many years of dedication and hard work. I can tell you from my own personal experience that as a doctor you will feel mentally challenged and emotionally fulfilled. I hope this book will clear an easier path to your goals and help you become an excellent physician. Good luck!

R. Stephen Toyos, M.D.

Introduction

"*A journey of a thousand miles must begin with a single step.*"

—*Lao-Tzu*

The first step in becoming a physician has nothing to do with choosing the right classes, school, professors or review books. The first step is to decide that you want to dedicate yourself to the profession. When you decide to become a doctor, essentially you are committing at least 11 years of your life to training. Most physicians have completed four years of undergraduate college, four years of medical school and then three to seven years of training in their respective specialty (like pediatrics, internal medicine, radiology, etc.). During the course of my training I have met some doctors who have told me, "If I knew what I was getting myself into, I would have never have become a doctor." I don't want you to say that after your training. This book will help you decide if medicine is for you. Once you have decided to become a doctor, this book will help you secure a position and excel in medical school. You have embarked on a long journey and this book will be the map that will help you successfully navigate from student to doctor.

Get to Know the Field

First meet with a physician and ask him or her what he or she does on a day-to-day basis. If you believe the Hollywood version of the medical profession, you probably think all physicians carry a stethoscope, save lives in a matter of minutes, see only about two patients a day, and deliver babies in the streets in their off hours. Being a physician has little to do with what you see on television. Many different types of physicians spend their work hours completing many different tasks. But do not take someone else's word for it. Ask a doctor if you can watch her work for a couple days. If the doctor works in private practice, then you can round out your exposure to the field by also spending time with a hospital-based physician. Observe physicians in different specialties. A good way to establish contact with physicians is by joining the volunteer program at the local hospital. Ask the program director if you could work closely with the physicians.

By receiving some exposure to medicine, you will begin to change any misconceptions and form an educated opinion about why you want to be a doctor. Also, when you are in a medical school interview, you will be able to answer the inevitable question, "Why do you want to be doctor?" The answer given by most people is, "I wanted a profession that combined my love for helping people with my interest in science." Not a bad canned answer, but think of how much more interesting your interview would be if you described your days working with physicians and how, through your exposure, you knew that you would love to emulate them.

What Are Your Chances of Getting into Medical School?

When I lecture to premedical students, they ask this most frequently. If you want stats, I'll give you stats, but remember: Do not let the numbers discourage you. One student, upon walking into his first chemistry class, heard his professor's ominous prediction that one out of every three of his students would fail the class. The student looked to his right and saw his high school's valedictorian; he looked to his left and saw a student with an honor society pin. He assumed that he would be the one out of three to fail, so he dropped the class.

Do not look at the numbers and decide you will fail. If your dream is to become a doctor and you work hard, your chances of entering medical school will defy the numbers. The fact that you are looking to this book for strategies is already helping you defy the odds of failing and increase the chances of realizing your dream.

The medical school freshman class of 1996 included 46,591 applications and 17,357 acceptances: an applicant-to- acceptance ratio of 7:2.

Of the total, 68 percent were first time applicants; 19 percent had applied previously; and 13 percent had applied at least twice previously. Applicants applied to, on average, 13 schools. Women composed 42 percent of the applications, and 37 percent of those women were accepted. Men composed 58 percent of the applicants, and 36 percent of men were accepted. Minorities (African-Americans, Native American/Alaskan Natives, Mexican-Americans, and mainland Puerto Ricans) composed 11 percent of the applicant pool, and 40 percent of those students were accepted. Asian/Pacific Islanders made up 20 percent of the applicant pool, and 32 percent were accepted. Other Hispanics made up 3.2 percent of the applicant pool, and 35 percent were accepted. I include these statistics because students always ask me for them, but no assumptions about your chances should be made from these numbers. Each application and circumstance is unique and class percentages may fluctuate from year to year.

Admission Criteria of the Students Accepted

The mean premedical grade point average was 3.4 using a standard 4.0 scale. The mean average for the Medical College Admission Test (MCAT), which is required by 121 of the medical schools, is divided into the three scores, one for each subsection of the test. Each of the following average scores for 1995 was out of a possible 15 points: The mean verbal reasoning score was 9.5; the mean physical sciences score was 9.7; the mean biological sciences score was 9.8. All of these scores were increases from the mean scores in 1994.

Public medical schools filled 89 percent of their classes with their own state residents. Private medical schools filled 44 percent of their classes with state residents. (Individual statistics of in-state and out-of-state entrants can be found in Appendix 1.)

Finally, 87 percent of the incoming class had completed a baccalaureate degree; 7 percent had a master's degree, and 2 percent had a doctoral degree.

These statistics change very little from year to year. Keep in mind that these are averages (bordered by students who did better and worse than the mean). Again, don't let them discourage you. Read on to find out how you can make yourself one of the fortunate ones to be accepted into medical school.

Which Schools Should You Consider?

After you have had a glimpse of the profession and you've decided you still want to become a doctor, your next question will likely be "Which school?" There are currently 125 medical schools in the United States and Puerto Rico, and they all have specific requirements for admission. (Refer to Appendix 1 for each school's requirements, or purchase a copy of the Medical School Admission Requirements, published by the Association of American Medical Colleges.) Appendix 1 lists all of these medical schools, along with a telephone number, Internet site, admission requirements, and other pertinent information for each.

Of course, applying to medical school requires time and money. Think back to the undergraduate college application process. Remember all the work and money that went into your application? Applying to medical school requires 10 times more time and effort. The next chapter shows you how to use a Strength of Candidate worksheet and a medical school ranking list to help you decide which schools you should apply to. You will not be applying to all these schools because that would be a waste of time and money.

Part 1

Chapter 1

The Application Process: AMCAS

You should consider your application as the first impression that you are making to the medical school. The first impression that you want to project is one of responsibility and dedication. Therefore you should devote enough time to the application so that it is neat, well thought out, and 100 percent correct. Most students take about three months completing their application.

The process of applying to medical school has been simplified by American Medical College Application Service (AMCAS), which provides a uniform application that is photocopied and sent to the schools of your choice by AMCAS. Of the 125 schools, 111 accept AMCAS applications. The others require their own applications. Appendix 1 identifies the schools that accept AMCAS. To receive an AMCAS application, contact your pre-medical counselor or write to:

> American Medical College Application Service
> Association of American Medical Colleges (AAMC)
> Section for Student Services
> 2450 N Street NW, Suite 201
> Washington, DC 20037-1131
> 202-828-0600

You should arrange to have all applications you need five months before you apply. Allow time for getting letters of recommendation and transcripts, and for preparing your personal statements. As soon as you receive your application, make two copies of each page, and place the original in a safe place. Do all of your preliminary work on the copies; only when you are 100 percent sure that you are ready to submit the application should you complete the original. Remember to make copies of any papers you will be sending to schools. Send the original papers.

To save you even more time, the AMCAS application is now available in computer form (AMCAS-E) for electronic transmission

Writing Your Personal Statement

The personal statement is a time to let the admissions committee know more about you. You will be given one full page to express yourself. Most students believe that the personal statement makes or breaks their application so they spend the majority of their time working on the personal statement and not on the rest of the application. During the admissions process the personal statement is usually read after your application has gone through a preliminary screening process that takes into account grades, MCAT (Medical College Admissions Test), and extracurricular activities. At that point, the personal statement may or may not be read. The time that the personal statement is read is by the interviewer before he interviews you. So a great personal statement alone will never get you into medical school. But a bad personal statement may sway an interviewer to reject you which may cost you a place in that year's medical school class.

The best and worst approaches

First I will explain what not to do in your personal statement and then I will describe some techniques that have led to excellent personal statements. You should not do something out of the ordinary with your personal statement. The medical field is a conservative profession. If you were applying for a school of arts, you might consider drawing a picture on the one allotted page for your personal statement. But for medical school, the personal statement should tell the school about you and why you want to be a doctor. Sounds simple. But many an applicant has tried the "let's show them how special we are in our personal statement" approach only to find that it receives a negative response. For example, a student did draw a picture that filled his one page for the personal statement. The picture showed him caring for a patient. The question asked by the admissions committee was, "Does this picture tell us about the person?" As one committee member stated, "The only thing that the drawing tells us is that he has some artistic ability but doesn't tell us what kind of physician he will be." Here are a few basic tips for writing an effective personal statement.

First, you should not be the only one reading the drafts of your personal statement. Since physicians will be reading your final version on the application, have physicians read your rough and final drafts. If you volunteer at a hospital, ask physicians you've gotten to know to read your statement.

Second, do not let your political or religious views come out in your personal statement. The physicians reviewing your application assume you have political and religious beliefs. But they want to know if you are capable of caring for the sick. Don't use the personal statement as a personal soap box. Stay away from polarized issues.

Third, do not think longer is better. The admissions committee reads thousands of applications a year. Admissions officers (made up of medical school faculty and deans of medical school, and sometimes students) want your information in a matter of minutes. Go beyond that time limit, and they will put your statement down and go to another.

Finally, your statement should be neat, without grammatical or spelling errors. Just as in grammar school, neatness counts. As one dean of a medical school explained to me, "If (applicants) are not going to pay attention to detail and turn in sloppy applications, they must not really want to be in medical school."

Tips for writing your personal statement

Start the process of writing your personal statement by brainstorming. Consider the following questions:

- Why do I want to be a physician?
- Who are my role models and why?
- What are my strengths, and how will I use them in my medical career?
- What distinguishes me from other applicants?
- What extracurricular activities have shown me the value of helping others?
- What are my future goals? How will a medical degree help me to meet these goals?

After you've rewritten the statement many times with a physician's assistance and you have a final draft, then take it to a professional writer. Many resume services will, for a nominal fee, check your statement for grammatical and spelling errors and then format the statement neatly on your application.

Letters of Recommendation

Letters from teaching assistants are not valuable. Letters from friends, clergy, relatives, and social group directors do not carry weight. Your college professors should write your recommendation letters. Also, if you have worked with a physician as a volunteer, researcher, or in any capacity, and he or she can write a strong letter, ask for it. That recommendation will be one of your best.

Professors and physicians are busy people, so ask them early in the process for a letter. Also, before asking for a letter, have your curriculum vitae (CV) available for the letter-writer. (See page 23 for a sample CV.) A CV will provide information the letter-writer may want to include in the letter of recommendation. Finally, give your letter-writers a date when the letter should be completed. Most undergraduate colleges have a Student Affairs Office where professors send their completed letters of recommendation. The office will send the letter to the addresses given by you. The office usually has a form where the professor will write his letter of recommendation. On the form, there will be a section where you can waive your right to see the completed letter. If you do not waive your right and see the letter, it will be so noted on the letter when it is sent. Medical school admissions committees do not like letters that the student has read because they feel that the letter-writer did not have total freedom to write how he or she really feels about you. So you should waive your right to read the letter. If you are unsure that a letter-writer will be able to write a strong letter, simply ask him or her. The writer should state emphatically that he or she can write you a strong letter.

Other Critical Parts of the Application

Many applicants spend far more time on the personal statement than any other part of the application. But attention to a few other sections could make the difference between an interview and a rejection. Most schools' admissions committees read only the personal statements of applications that pass preliminary screening.

The most overlooked sections of the AMCAS application are the Post-Secondary Honors/Awards, the Extracurricular Activities, and the Volunteer Activities/Employment sections. During preliminary screening, you can receive points for particular jobs, awards, volunteer work, and activities. (A general idea of which activities receive points is covered in the Strength of Candidate Section later in this book.). These sections, more so than the personal statement, can make the difference between an interview or a rejection. The reason being is an admissions officer may find an activity in which you have participated that he can relate to. For example, if you volunteer as a counselor for the Boy Scouts

Sample CV

Sara Thomas
475 North Westerbrook
Chicago, Illinois 57432
(219)-555-5555

EDUCATION: Northsouthern University, Ellis, Illinois
Senior English Major, Graduation 1995

EXPERIENCE: Tutor—Chicago Upward Bound Program for
Disadvantaged Youth, 1993 to present
Volunteer—Manning Hospital, 1993 to present
Researcher—Analysis of the Effects of Cimetidine
on Rat Digestive Tract, Barr Research
Laboratories, 1991 to 1993
Faculty Advisor—Camp Caz Youth Camp,
Summer of 1990

**EXTRACURRICULAR
ACTIVITIES:** Vice-President—Northsouthern Premedical Society,
1992 to present
Representative—Northsouthern School Council,
1990 to 1993
Exchange Student—Argentina exchange program,
gained fluency in Spanish, 1992
Honors: First Place—Northsouthern Annual Poetry
Contest "Wings", 1991

**ADDITIONAL
INFORMATION:** Participant—Northsouthern intramural sports
Enjoy—opera, gourmet cooking, and reading books
by Spanish authors

of America, maybe the officer will find that interesting enough to grant you an interview or better if that person is involved in the same organization. A simple connection of affiliation with the same group may secure an interview to a school that would not normally give your application a second thought. These sections give the admissions committee a quick look at what you have achieved without spending half an hour digging the information out from your personal statement.

Another part of the application asks you to calculate your grade point averages (GPA). This section is straightforward, but check your calculations carefully.

Your MCAT score is the most important score (besides your GPA) medical colleges will consider in your application. The MCAT is the medical school entrance exam, and the next chapter covers it in detail.

Selecting Medical Schools

The last section of the AMCAS application is one of the most important: picking the schools to which you will send applications. I will answer the most frequently-asked questions about school selection. The main question that you must ask yourself is "Is my main objective to be a doctor or to be in a certain area of the world?"

Medical school admission is very competitive. Do not limit yourself by saying, "I will go only here." Your goal should be becoming a physician. A large number of medical school applicants apply simply based on location. If they do not receive a spot in the location they want, they decide not to go that year and apply again the following year. These students may or may not end up in their choice location even after waiting for a year. I have found, in talking to some of these applicants, that they eventually realize that location doesn't matter and that being a doctor is their number one priority.

How many schools should you apply to?

I have a friend who, all through college, talked about applying only to medical schools close enough to beaches where he could surf. He was one of the highest-ranked students in our class. During the application process he sent his application to three schools close to a surfing beach. We thought he would have no trouble getting in, especially because one of the schools did not have a high ranking (ranking discussed below). Well, he was not accepted and waited one full year before being accepted to medical school. In the end he did not go to a school close to the surf. No matter who you are, three schools is too few.

How many schools is enough?

The number of schools to which you should apply depends on your strength as a candidate. The weaker a candidate you are, the more schools you should apply to. We'll get into specific numbers shortly, but in general, do not limit your choices due to financial considerations. The extra money needed to apply to a few more schools is small compared to the time and money you would spend reapplying.

How Do You Judge Your Strength as a Candidate?

Most schools have tried to make the selection process fair by assigning points for specific criteria during preliminary screening. Usually if you pass preliminary screening, school officials then review your personal statement, letters of recommendation, and information from interviews. Here's a system used for assigning points similar to that being used by some medical schools.

Science GPA and MCAT scores are traditionally the two most important criteria. First, if you have mostly As in your science courses, give yourself six points. If you have mostly Bs, give yourself four. If you have Bs and Cs, give yourself two points.

For the MCATs, if you have a combined score of average or below (using the national average), give yourself two points. If your score is above average, give yourself four. If your score is comfortably above average, give yourself six.

Next, rank your current school. If it's in the top 25 according to *U.S. News and World Report*, give yourself a three. If it is a top-50 school, give yourself a two. For any other school, give yourself a one.

If you have a graduate degree, give yourself an extra point. Add an extra point also for any of the following: you have done publishable research; you have extraordinary experience, such as any job that serves the public; you are an underrepresented minority (African-American, Mexican-American, Puerto Rican, Native American); or you participated in extracurricular activities (school government, sports, music, volunteer group).

These are basic criteria and sample point values. Some schools have others; for example, if you commit to being a physician in a rural area for a few years, some schools add a point.

Add your score. If your score is 21 to 15, apply to at least nine schools. If your score is between 15 and 10, apply to at least 15 schools. If you have a score below 10, apply to at least 20 schools.

Strength of Candidate Calculation Sheet

Criteria	Score
GPA:	
Mostly *A*s = 6 points	_____
*A*s and *B*s = 4 points	_____
*B*s and *C*s = 2 points	_____
MCAT composite score:	
10 points higher than nat. avg. = 6 points	_____
Six points higher than nat. avg. = 4 points	_____
National Average or below = 2 points	_____
Undergraduate School Strength:	
Top 25 = 3 points	_____
Top 50 = 2 points	_____
All others = 1 point	_____
One point for each category:	
Graduate Degree	_____
Research	_____
Public Service Job	_____
Underrepresented Minority	_____
Special Awards	_____
Extracurricular Activity	_____
TOTAL SCORE	_____

Which Schools Should You Apply to?

Apply to all the schools in your state of residence because the government mandates state schools to take a certain percentage of state residents. Also, apply to the private institutions of your state; they may also give preferential treatment to residents even though it is not mandated. Staying close to home for medical school is generally not a bad idea anyway: Your friends and family will be there to provide moral support.

You should also apply to medical schools that have historically taken graduates from your undergraduate college. Ask your premedical advisor who has counseled students before you where former graduates have gone. If your school does not have a premedical advisor, ask the professors who teach the prerequisite premedical school courses. They would know where the students for whom they have written letters of recommendation have gone to medical school.

Divide the rest of your choices according to the categories below. This ranking system was developed by a residency selection committee. You may find another ranking system in *The Gourman Report : A rating of Graduate and Professional Programs* by Dr. Jack Gourman in cooperation with National Educational Standards. (Look for it in your local library.) The reason for dividing the choices between the three categories below is that throughout the years, I have noticed that some students self select themselves from applying to the higher level ranked schools because they feel they do not have a chance. I have met many students who have been rejected by lower ranked schools only to gain acceptance in a top 10 school. Remember, you never know what might catch an admissions officer's eye. so apply to some top gun, excellent and strong schools.

TOP GUNS

Harvard Medical School
John Hopkins University
University of California, San Francisco
University of Pennsylvania
University of California, Los Angeles
Stanford University
Yale University

University of Michigan
University of Chicago
Washington University, St. Louis
Cornell University
Columbia University
Duke University
Vanderbilt University

EXCELLENT SCHOOLS

University of Rochester
New York University
University of Minnesota

Tulane University
Northwestern University
University of Illinois

EXCELLENT SCHOOLS (cont)

Boston University

University of California, San Diego

University of North Carolina

Indiana University

Tufts University

University of Iowa

Dartmouth Medical School

Georgetown University

University of Pittsburgh

University of Southern California

Ohio State University

University of Virginia

University of Washington

STRONG SCHOOLS

State University of New York at Stony Brook

University of California, Davis

University of California, Irvine

Albert Einstein College of Medicine

Baylor College of Medicine

University of Louisville

State University of New York at Buffalo

Temple University

Bowman Gray School of Medicine

Emory University

Brown University Program in Medicine

University of Missouri

Wayne State

George Washington University

GOOD SCHOOLS

All other medical schools in the nation are considered good as compared to medical schools in other countries. A medical degree from the United States means more in the U.S. than a degree from the best medical school in another country.

Keep in mind that some schools have certain departments that merit a higher ranking than the school in general merits. For example, you may want to be an orthopedic surgeon. Say you end up at a school whose orthopedic department is considered one of the best. When applying for a residency position in orthopedics, you will have an advantage over most students from higher ranking schools because your exposure to the field is better, and good letters from highly respected physicians can gain you a top residency position.

Does It Matter Where You Go to School?

It matters where you go to school. But no one school will fulfill every student's needs. For example, if your dream is to become an academic physician, you're better off attending a school that has research opportunities for medical students. You want not only the exposure to research but, when applying for residency positions, a better chance of obtaining a spot. Another reality that is often downplayed when applying to medical schools but changes when applying for residency is the ranking of the school. I talked with a physician who sat on a residency admissions panel who stated, "If we had a choice between an honor student from a highly ranked school and an honor student from a school ranked in the bottom third we would take the student from the 'good school'." The statement may not seem fair to a school or a student, but some medical schools have earned a reputation for graduating top notch physicians and that reputation adds to a perceived quality of their graduates. Some programs use medical schools' ranking as one of the criteria in judging residency applicants.

Does this mean you should go to the highest ranked school possible? No, no, no. A highly ranked school is only one criteria that residency coordinators use when picking residents. Be aware of rankings, but consider other points as well.

Will the School Offer an Adequate Support System?

Medical school requires a tremendous amount of work, and you will feel pressure. To help relieve the pressure, look to good friends, family, classmates, activities in the community, and support from the school. Will your choice of school support you by providing adequate study facilities, review sessions, planned extracurricular activities, physician and student advisors, and an accessible student affairs office? Will the school you choose offer one of these support systems through close proximity to friends and relatives?

Will the Cost of Attending Your First Choice Further Increase the Pressure?

The national average loan debt for each graduating class is around $60,000. I interviewed students who will graduate with twice or three times that amount. Some of these students had choices to go to less expensive schools. These large debts have caused anxiety in these students, and if they had the process to do over, they say they might have gone to less expensive schools. Financial considerations begin to play a role in specialty choice, location of practice, type of practice, and choosing between an academic career or a private practice track.

There are ways, besides loans, to pay for medical school. If you are attending a public college, one simple way to cut medical school costs is to become a state resident. State residents pay about half the tuition than out-of-state students. The criteria for becoming a state resident varies from state to state. You can live in some states less than three months, receive a driver's license, and register to vote to be considered a resident. In the summer before medical school, you could move to the state where you are going to attend school and attain resident status. Some students have also used this technique to increase their chances of acceptance in state schools that primarily take state residents.

Some schools offer tuition waivers in exchange for research. You devote a certain number of hours a week during the school year or spend the summer of your first year in the lab in exchange for a tuition-free year.

The government has programs sponsored by the Health Resources and Services Administration and Public Health Service that offer money to medical students in exchange for practicing medicine in certain designated areas for a specified time. For example, to pay your tuition for four years of medical school, you could owe three years of service to an Indian reservation taking care of the inhabitants.

The armed forces offer tuition and stipends in exchange for military commitment upon completion of a residency. Most of the time for every year of medical school tuition paid, the armed forces expects one year of active duty after your residency. During active duty, you would be stationed at a base where you would take care of soldiers and their families. Other special arrangements exist, so ask the recruiter for all the possibilities available.

The National Institute of Health has the Howard Hughes Medical Institute which pays medical students for one year of research. In this program, medical students who have completed two years of medical school apply for research positions. If chosen, you spend one year completing research with a mentor while earning a salary. Once the year is complete, you would then continue your medical school education.

Finally, each medical school offers scholarships to qualified students. During an interview trip to the school, always stop by the financial aid office and ask them about scholarships. Also ask the medical students showing you the campus about available scholarships or work.

You should write or call all programs on this list and see what opportunities are available. Remember, you are under no obligation, so it does not hurt to learn about all your options.

Hughes Fellowship Program
The Fellowship Office
National Research Council
2101 Constitution Ave.
Washington, DC 20418
202-334-2872

Howard Hughes Medical Institute
Office of Grants and Special Programs
Department PO 95
4000 Jones Bridge Rd.
Chevy Chase, MD 20815-6789
301-215-8889

National Health Service Corps
Scholarship Program
U.S. Public Health Recruitment
8201 Greensboro Dr.
Suite 600
Mclean, VA 22102

Air Force
Medical Recruiting Division
HQ USAFRS/RSHM
550 D St. West, Suite 1
Randolph AFB, TX 78150-4527

Army
U.S. Army Health
Professions Support Agency SGPS-PD
5109 Leesburg Pike
Falls Church, VA 22041-3258

Navy
Commander, Navy
Recruiting Command
801 North Randolph
Arlington, VA 22203-1991

Student Guide, 1993-94
Department of Education
Federal Student Aid Information Center
P.O. Box 84
Washington, DC 20044
1-800-4-FED AID

Minority students have additional resources. If you are Black American, Native American, Mexican-American/Chicano, or Puerto Rican, you are considered an underrepresented minority. These students make up 8.1 percent of the total student population.

1995-96 Percent of Total Enrollment

Black American	9.0
Native American	0.9
Mexican-American	3.1
Mainland Puerto Rican	0.7

The AAMC (Association of American Colleges) has a program to circulate biographical information to the minority affairs offices of all U.S. Medical Schools. The service will distribute information similar to the information found in your AMCAS application. Minority Affairs officers are always recruiting minorities to their schools. Some schools offer financial assistance to try to entice outstanding students to enroll in their school. This service costs you nothing. The program is called the Medical Minority Applicant Registry (Med-Mar). For more information write to:

Minority Student Information Clearinghouse
Division of Minority Health, Education and Prevention
Association of American Medical Colleges
2450 N. St., NW
Washington, DC 20037-1126

Minority students may write to request information about financial aid, study strategies, career development, and career opportunities. All information is free. Send a letter to:

Office of Statewide Health Planning and Development
Health Professions Career Opportunity Program
1600 Ninth St., Room 441
Sacramento, CA 95814

These schools have historically actively recruited and enrolled a high percentage of minority students as compared to other U.S. medical schools. If you meet the criteria of a minority applicant, you should strongly consider applying to these schools to increase your chances of getting into medical school.

TOP SCHOOLS for Minority Enrollment*
Univ. of California, Davis
Univ. of California, Los Angeles (includes Drew)
Univ. of California, San Francisco
Univ. of Southern California
Harvard University
Howard University**
Univ. of Illinois
Meharry University**
Univ. of Michigan
Morehouse University**
Univ. of Medicine and Dentistry of New Jersey
    Robert Wood Johnson

State University of New York , Brooklyn
Temple University
Univ. of Texas , Dallas
Univ. of Texas , Galveston
Univ. of Texas , San Antonio

  *Compiled with the help of Minority Affairs officers and counselors
**African-American colleges; any student may apply

Do All Medical Schools Offer the Same Curriculum?

Years ago, all medical schools followed a standard curriculum. The first two years were spent in lecture and in learning anatomy, physiology, pathology, microbiology, biochemistry, behavioral science, pharmacology, and histology. Toward the end of the second year, students took a class in history and physical diagnosis, where they would learn basic examination skills. The third and last years of medical school were devoted to hospital work in the different areas of medicine, such as internal medicine or pediatrics. This was the traditional curriculum.

Now some schools have adopted a different curriculum and pedagogy. There are many different names for this new approach, but most schools call it Problem-Based Learning (PBL). Harvard adopted this system, and public television has shown a running documentary called "So you want to be a doctor?" following the lives of students going through this new curriculum.

PBL attempts to integrate all of medicine's facts and skills using a series of different medical histories. For example, instead of teaching anatomy as a subject separate from pathology, a physician/professor presents the history of a patient to a group of 10 medical students and then leads a discussion about the anatomy, physiology, biochemistry, pathology, and pharmacology of the patient's condition. Most schools that adopt this type of curriculum have retained the traditional lecture format for various subjects. On the other hand, medical students are exposed early on to the way physicians think, solve problems, and care for patients. Some schools have students, accompanied by physicians, seeing patients the first month.

Some schools offer an independent study program (ISP). In an ISP you develop your own curriculum. Some schools require successful completion of all medical school exams but will not require attendance to lectures and labs. Some students use the extra time to do research or accompany physicians at a hospital. Some students plan educational trips and clerkships to other medical schools. These programs are recommended only for the student who is highly motivated and disciplined.

There are advantages and disadvantages to both the traditional and the new curricula. With the new curriculum (either PBL or ISP), most students like the fact that they are learning about medicine immediately instead of waiting until the end of the second year. Some students, though, feel they are getting a gestalt of medicine but not learning the pre-clinical subjects in depth.

With the traditional curriculum, some students feel they are not in medical school, but graduate school since patient contact and medical problem-solving is minimal. On the positive side, students feel they have a strong background in pre-clinical subjects. I have seen great physicians trained in either format. The one common denominator great physicians have is a strong work ethic. So whatever curriculum you choose, if you apply yourself you should end up a competent physician.

What Special Educational Programs are Available in Medical School?

Some medical schools offer joint-degree programs. The most common dual degree is the MD/Ph.D., which is offered by 111 medical colleges. Most of these programs offer full-tuition waivers to students completing the MD/Ph.D. Also, some of these programs are funded by the National Institutes of Health, and the program is titled the Medical Scientist Training Program (MSTP). MSTP graduates have a high success rate in attaining NIH research grants once in practice.

Joint MD and Masters of Public Health degree programs are offered by 32 schools. Twelve schools offer a joint MD/JD (Doctor of Jurisprudence). Sixteen schools offer a joint MD/MBA (Master of Business Administration). In the future, more physicians will be involved not in direct patient care, but in the business, legal, and political aspects of medicine.

Call or write for more information:

Program Administrator
Medical Scientist Training Program
Room 905, Westwood Building
National Institutes of Health
Bethesda, MD 20892
301-594-7744

How Do you Find Out What a School Has to Offer?

First, telephone each school you are considering, and ask them to send you information about the school (Appendix 1). They will send you a brochure about the school and how to apply. (Again, most schools will accept AMCAS applications, but some require their own.) From the brochure, you'll get a general idea about the school and the location.

Second, to really find out about a school, talk to current students there. Your college should have a list of recent graduates who have gone to medical school. Call those students and ask them what they think of their schools. If you cannot identify students from your own under-graduate college, call medical schools you're interested in and ask to talk with some of their current students. You may receive a biased set of opinions using the latter method because schools may not give you the names of dissatisfied students. Overall, I have found students to be honest about the strengths and weaknesses of their schools.

What is the Early Decision Program (EDP)?

In 1996, 88 AAMC medical schools participated in the EDP. Here's how the program works. First, you apply to only one medical school by mid-August. The school informs you of acceptance or rejection by October 1. If accepted, you are obligated to attend that medical school. If rejected, you still have time to apply to the other schools and, if you wish, reapply to the school that rejected you. Reapplying to your first choice may make sense: The school that rejected you may, after review-ing the rest of the applicant pool, decide you deserve a place.

Admissions officers have stated that borderline students gain no advantage by applying through the EDP because they usually only accept strong candidates that they know would be accepted into their school during the normal application process. Great candidates also do not gain an advantage because they will generally be accepted whether they utilize EDP or the regular route. The one advantage EDP offers is early notification about where you'll go to medical school. Also, you save time, money, and energy by foregoing secondary applications and interviews at other schools. If one school stands out above the rest for you, apply through EDP. If you have unanswered questions that can be answered with more time, utilize the regular application procedure.

Many students do not take full advantage of all the opportunities available to them. Before applying, explore all options even if you don't think they are right for you because until completely informed, you can-not rule out an option. The more you prepare and plan at this stage of the application process, the better your chances of acceptance and suc-cessful completion of medical school.

Chapter 2

The Medical College Aptitude Test (MCAT)

From the Strength of Candidate sheet, you can see that the MCAT is as important as your undergraduate GPA. The MCAT has become so important because some undergraduates have been accused of grade inflation. The only way a medical school can tell if an A student at school X is as good as an A student at school Y is by giving them the same test and comparing their scores. If you have had an average undergraduate academic record, a good score on the MCAT could improve your chances of acceptance.

Taking the Medical College Aptitude Test (MCAT)

The MCAT, the medical school entrance exam, takes a full eight-hour day to complete. It has four parts: verbal reasoning, physical sciences, writing sample, and biological sciences. The maximum score for each section is 15, and the average score is 7 to 8. The writing sample section is the exception. It is scored by a letter grade.

The table below shows the number of questions, total time allotted, number of seconds you theoretically have for each question, and the scoring scale used for each section.

Section	Number of Questions	Time Allotted	Time per Question	Score
Verbal Reasoning	65	85 min	40 sec	1-15
Physical Sciences	77	100 min	1 min 14 sec	1-15
Essay	2	60 min	30 min	J-T
Biological Sciences	77	100 min	1 min 14 sec	1-15

Most schools add these points to give a composite score. If you score average on one section but above average on another, those extra points will help you. A good composite score, even with a low score in one section, may be good reason not to retake the exam: you could do worse the second time around. So decide carefully.

The MCAT is offered in April and August. Since most schools start accepting applications in June and stop in late November, they recommend that you take the April exam. I also recommend taking the April exam for three reasons. One, although schools process your application file when they receive it, admissions offices hold it for consideration until they receive your MCAT scores. The earlier you complete your application file, i.e., provide your MCAT scores and required recommendations, the earlier a school will consider you for an interview, giving you a jump on your competition. Two, you will be able to focus your energies on your application (AMCAS) and secondaries (individual applications from schools) during the summer. Three, if you are not satisfied with your scores, you can retake the exam in August.

The prerequisites for the MCAT are physics, general chemistry, organic chemistry, and biology. Consider these courses preparation for the MCAT, and take them very seriously. Two other courses that I highly recommend before the MCAT are physiology and biochemistry.

The MCAT can be taken a maximum of three times unless you have a valid reason to take it a fourth. Prepare for it as though it is one of the most important tests you will ever take, because it is.

Studying for the MCAT

The majority of premeds preparing for the MCAT start studying four to five months before the test. The reason for such an early start is that most students are taking other course work simultaneously. I believe that four to five months' study time is appropriate and satisfactory to do well on the test. Again, work hard in the prerequisites (biology, physics, etc.) so your MCAT preparation will be easier.

Before studying, determine an approach for conquering the MCAT. First decide if you are disciplined enough to study on your own. If not, you may want to take a course to guide you through the process. If you decide to take one of the MCAT courses (Kaplan, Princeton Review, Columbia, etc.), register early, obtain the materials they offer, and review them before the course actually starts. For example, if you plan to take the April MCAT and also take a review course, register for the course before winter break and get the review books they offer ahead of time. Then, during break, get familiar with the materials. Although no one likes studying during vacation, getting a position in a medical school takes a few sacrifices.

When gathering materials, consult others who have taken the test to find the better guides. The MCAT prep guide, offered by the AAMC, is an essential resource. It is relatively inexpensive and published by the association that writes the MCAT. (It will give you a taste of the actual exam.) This MCAT prep guide packet includes an outline guide of all the topics the MCAT could possibly cover and a few full-length tests. Use the outline provided as you begin to study. Save the tests for after your thorough review.

You can also use old notes, course texts, published MCAT review guides (a text written by Flowers has been recommended by many students). If you purchase a published guides, choose carefully. Some guides turn out to be a waste of time and money. A friend of mine warned me of an expensive book that boasted a thorough review of every section of the MCAT and six full-length tests. When studying the guide, he found many errors including an incorrect definition of osmolality. He quickly became uncomfortable with any information the book presented and had to buy a different book and start his review from scratch.

To help you be psychologically prepared for the test, I suggest reserving a few Saturdays or Sundays to take full-length tests. Recruit a friend also taking the MCAT, and simulate aspects of the test, from getting up at 7:30 in the morning to sticking to the time allotment for each section. After taking the test, score each other, and discuss the testing strategies that worked. Mock exams will help you feel much more comfortable when the day of reckoning actually arrives.

A Closer Look at the MCAT

Part 1: Verbal Reasoning

The section of the MCAT that gives many students difficulty is the verbal reasoning section. This is the first section you'll take. It uses passages with comprehension questions to test the ability to read quickly with suitable comprehension. Medical colleges find this very important. However, many students do not study for verbal reasoning and do poorly. The subject matter of the passages is not scientific information. Instead, the passages focus on humanities topics such as philosophy, history, and sociology. Although there is no specific study material to help you improve answering the questions, practicing old tests will better your score.

The first few times you practice taking the test, try new approaches until you feel comfortable with a particular approach. Then stick with that method and refine it. One method that might work for you is reading the first paragraph, then the last paragraph, and then the questions. Another method is to first briefly review the questions, read the whole passage rapidly, and then answer the questions. Or just read the whole passage right off, and then answer the questions. It is hard to say which method works the best. The key is to determine the best strategy for you, and practice using that strategy.

The types of questions asked on the verbal reasoning test not only whether you gathered all the facts, but whether you can assimilate the information and understand the author's point of view. Inference is a key skill that will bolster your score.

Here is an example of a verbal reasoning passage and some questions that might follow it. You should not take more than five minutes to finish the passage and questions.

Before the 20th century, military strength provided for the success of a nation. From the Mongolian dominance of Eurasia to the Spanish Armada's command of colonization, military power was the primary factor of supremacy. A clear example of military dominance leading to the success of a nation is the French Army of Napoleon. For the first time in history, the entire economy was converted into a war machine. The powerful French army pressed on neighboring borders in all directions making France one of the most powerful nations in the world.

A steady transformation manifested itself during the Cold War era that debilitated military strength and placed global power in the pocket. At the onset of the indirect war with the U.S., the Soviet Union built its military to be the voice of the republic. However, its armed forces became a vacuum leaching the communist economy and included itself in the list of dominating factors leading to the crippled and fragmented commonwealth. The U.S.S.R. provides the archetype illustrating the withering importance of the military and the increasing economic environment.

The ascendance of post-World War II Japan and West Germany to positions of power are additional examples of the altered importance of the military. Japan, depleted by its efforts in the greatest war, changed its focus from a military to an economy. Despite the claim that the limitations and guaranteed protection forced on Japan in 1945 by the U.S. afforded Japan its present economic fortitude, Japan is a member of today's major powers because of its economic resources and not its military.

Although Israel initially seemed to support the quintessential military, it provides a further illustration of economic power overwhelming military strength. This Jewish state depended on the strength of its military to fend off the aggressive Muslim periphery. For example, during the Six Day War in

1967, a largely outnumbered Israeli army overcame the enemy, ensuring Israel's survival. For the incessantly threatened nation, survival equals success. So by simple logic, this nation's success is determined by military prowess, not economic vigor. However, this logic may not hold true. The U.S. provides Israel with many of the technological advantages and moneys needed to nurture such a lethal military. Since the U.S. is providing this economic aid, it supports the impression that currency provides the successful shield.

Whereas the U.S. economic aid provides for the economic foundation of military power in Israel, Iraq shows that the military is impotent. Iraq actualized one of the largest standing armies in the world at the time of the Persian Gulf War. In a region of military recreants, Iraq could have potentially expanded to superpower contention. However, today's increasingly civilized world does not tolerate expansion of power by force. Iraq was defeated by globally united enemies.

Deterring the origin of a nation's success is difficult. The economy and military are interrelated, with one supporting the other. Nonetheless, in the post-Cold War world, the balance tipped generously towards economic strength as the foundation for a nation's welfare.

1. According to the author, Iraq's success in the Persian Gulf War was deterred by:

A. U.S. military support.

B. Iraq's lack of economic strength.

C. Rivals of Iraqi growth.

D. Opponents of Iraqi expansion methods.

2. The central idea of the passage is that:

A. The Post Cold War era is full of change.

B. Military strength is a prime factor in a nation's survival.

C. Economic power is the most important determinant of a nation's expansion.

D. There has been an alteration in the foundations of success and power.

3. In line 42, what is meant by the economic foundation of military power?

A. The armed forces are no longer important.

B. Military strength is subsidized by the economy.

C. Survival of a nation is dependent on the economy.

D. Israel's economy is the foundation of its strength.

4. According to the passage, which of the following are true.
  I.   Israel's strength was dependent on foreign favor.
  II. West Germany's success is a function of U.S. pressure.
  III. A nation's military is not a determinant of its strength.

  A. I and II
  B. I and III
  C. I only
  D. I , II, and III

This passage is not particularly difficult. Most of the information is straightforward and requires little inference. Passages found in the MCAT vary in difficulty, but the most challenging are the questions that require inference.

The answers are:
1. D 2. D 3. B 4. C

If you are reading this book before your junior year as an undergraduate, practice for your verbal reasoning section by reading difficult literature. Read from the humanities, especially scholarly journals with reviews and opinionated works.

Part II: Physical Sciences

This is the second section of the MCAT you will encounter, and it's a difficult 100 minutes. The 77 questions in this section test your training in general chemistry and physics. Some topics covered in this section are:

acids and bases	kinematics
gas laws	electromagnetism
thermodynamic laws	circuits
bonding	Newtonian Physics
periodic table	optics

Students studying for the MCAT often have two preconceptions about this section of the test.

First, some students have the preconception that this section tests your knowledge of these areas. For the old MCAT, that was true. The new MCAT, however, requires you to take unfamiliar information and answer questions by applying your knowledge in these areas. The science passages cover fundamental principles, for instance, but related to topics you're probably unfamiliar with. The objective here is to help schools gauge how well you can assimilate new scientific information, a skill that will be essential throughout your career as a physician.

The second preconception students often have about this section is that the science section requires many calculations and memorization of important formulas. In recent years, the MCAT has moved further and furter away from requiring students to recite formulas and perform calculations; it now instead tests your ability to think.

This section includes basically two types of questions: those related to a passage and those that stand alone. The questions tied to a passage are designed to test your ability to understand new information. Some of the answers can be found right in the passage or derived from information presented in the passage. Some of the questions related to a passage might require knowledge from your studies. The questions that stand alone require previous knowledge gained in your required pre-medical courses.

Here is an example of a physical sciences passage and its related questions. Take seven minutes to read it and answer the questions.

The bioavailabity of drugs is a crucial concern to pharmaceutical companies. For a drug taken orally, effective absorption occurs when the drug can move from the gastrointestinal tract, through a lipid barrier, into the plasma compartment.

Drugs can cross a lipid barrier when they are lipid soluble. Polar substances are not lipid soluble and remain in the GI tract. Nonpolar or nonionized substances can cross the lipid barrier into the blood plasma.

Determination of the form of a drug at a particular pH requires use of the Henderson-Hasselbach equation:

pH = pKa + log [A-]/[HA]

The rate at which the drug will be available is also of concern. According to Fick's Law:

rate= (C1-C2) X (Pc/Thickness) X Area

Pc, the permeability coefficient, is a function of the drug

C refers to the concentration each compartment

Drug A is a weak base (pKb = 4.4)
Drug B is a small hydrocarbon molecule
Drug C is an antacid
Drug D is an acid with a pKa of 5.0
Plasma pH = 7.4   Gastric Juice pH = 1.4

1. **In the stomach, what will be the dominant form of Drug A?**
   A. There will be an even mixture of ionized and nonionized form.
   B. Drug A is nonpolar in gastric juice, so the dominant form is absorbed.
   C. The dominant form is the protonated base.
   D. The dominant form is the nonionized form.

2. **Which one of the following is the most plausible reason why Drug B is found to be absorbed more in the small intestine than in the stomach?**
   A. Plasma flow through the intestine is much less, therefore creating a larger concentration gradient than the stomach.
   B. The hydrocarbon form of Drug B is degraded by the HCl in the stomach, leaving most of the absorption of intact drug to occur in the small intestine.
   C. The surface area of the small intestine is much greater than that of the stomach.
   D. Drug B cannot be absorbed because it is a polar molecule.

3. **A dose of Drug C, an antacid, increases the pH of the intestine by 1.6. What is the concentration of the hydroxide ion?**
   A. 10-11
   B. 10-3
   C. 103
   D Because the conditions are still acidic, there will not be any hydroxide ion.

4. **What is the pH of a 0.10 M solution of Drug D where:**
   AH <=> A- + H+
   A. 2.0
   B. 3.0
   C. 5.0
   D. 6.0

Did you notice that some answers come directly from information found in the passage?

Answers:

1) C. In an environment of pH 1.4, a weak base will be mostly protonated. Henderson-Hasselbalch can be used to calculate the exact ratio of protonated to unprotonated drug.

2) C. Fick's Law.

3) A. Using the relationship $[H+][OH-] = K_w = 1.00 \times 10^{-14}$
and $pH = \log(1/[H+])$

4) B. Using $K_a = [H+][A-]/[HA] = X^2/[.1-X] = 10^{-pKa}$ (eliminate denominator X, insignificant)

$10^{-pKa} = X^2/.1$

$X - 1 \times 10^{-3} = [H+]$

$pH = 3.0$

Some of the questions require calculation and previous knowledge of concepts to find the correct answer, but you should not have had to use a calculator. This brings up another important point. You cannot use a calculator on the MCAT. So you might as well start practicing your skills. Try using a calculator for your course work only when the math is difficult. When studying for the MCAT, your calculator should be nowhere in sight.

Part III: Writing Sample

The writing sample is an indication of your ability to communicate. Medical schools will expect you to effectively organize your ideas and explain your thoughts. In this section of the MCAT, you will be presented with two different statements and asked to 1) explain what the statement means, 2) present an example opposite to the statement, and 3) attempt to settle the difference between the two viewpoints. The topics are not controversial issues like racial discrimination or abortion; they are simple statements that offer ample opportunity for discussion.

Here is an example of a statement:

Man's incessant growth will lead to his death.

When you approach the writing sample, take an organized approach, and complete all three parts of the assignment. You will have a half hour to write on each of the two statements, for a total of an hour. For each statement, take the first few minutes to organize your thoughts into an outline.

Practicing writing samples can definitely improve your score. Team up with a friend also studying for the MCAT, write on the same topic from a practice test, and evaluate each other's samples. Topics from previous years' tests often reappear, so approach every practice as if it were the real thing, including timing yourselves.

Part IV: Biological Sciences

You'll get to this, the final section of the test, by late afternoon, and you'll probably be exhausted. However, most students are well-prepared for this section of the MCAT because of their course work.

The biological sciences section covers topics from biology and organic chemistry. Examples of topics are:

Biology

Physiological systems (cardiovascular, endocrine, and respiratory, etc.)

Cellular biology

Genetics

Evolution

Organic chemistry

Stereochemistry

Organic structures (amines, proteins, etc.)

Mechanisms

Laboratory

As in the physical science section, the biological sciences will cover fundamental principles, for instance, but related to topics you are unfamiliar with.

Here is an example of a passage and some questions you might encounter. Try to finish the questions in five minutes.

Respiration is the process of creating pressure differences in the thoracic cavity to provide perfusion of blood with oxygen and the release of carbon dioxide.

A major difficulty in understanding pulmonary mechanics is intrapleural pressure. Pleural fluid is found between the chest wall and the pleural surface of the lung. Intrapleural pressure is the negative pressure exerted on the pleural fluid by the expanding chest wall and elastic lung. With contraction, the diaphragm pulls downward, transferring pressure to the pleural fluid, which then transfers this pressure to the lungs, leading to decreased alveolar pressure.

Many problems can affect intrapleural pressure. A pneumothorax refers to air in the intrapleural space. Also, smokers with emphysema have an increased lung compliance, which affects intrapleural pressure. Compliance is the measure of change in volume over change in pressure.

1. In emphysema, a person's lung becomes less elastic. What effect on intrapleural pressure would this have?

A. More positive intrapleural pressure because the lung is stiffer.

B. More negative intrapleural pressure because the lung is more flexible.

C. More positive intrapleural pressure because the lung tissue is less elastic.

D. No change in pressure because emphysema affects compliance only.

2. Which of the following is true of lungs with constricted bronchial airways in contrast to lungs with normal airways?

A. Require a greater volume of air to inflate.

B. Need greater intrapleural pressure for the same volume of air.

C. Require a more compliant lung to inflate.

D. Rate of inflation is decreased.

3. A child with respiratory problems is suspected of having cystic fibrosis. Neither his father nor his mother has the disease. Which of the following cannot be true.

A. Cystic fibrosis is an autosomal recessive disease.

B. Cystic fibrosis is autosomal dominant with varying degrees of penetrance.

C. Cystic fibrosis arises from mutations in chromosome 7.

D. Cystic fibrosis is an X-linked dominant disease.

Answers
1. C 2. D 3. D

Final Tips for Succeeding with the MCAT

The MCAT is a long eight hours of complicated readings and difficult questions, yet many people spend the night before the test cramming in last minute details and exhausting themselves. Instead, relax the night before, and be sure to get a full night's rest. If you are taking the test at a distant location, travel there the day before to settle yourself. Reduce all possible sources of stress because the MCAT itself will provide plenty.

Also, take along a digital timer with which you have practiced. Then you will know if your rate is on target for each passage or question. If you're nervous enough that any noise in the testing room could break your concentration, take ear plugs. But be sure you've used them during your practice testing so they won't seem foreign and make you feel uncomfortable during the test.

For MCAT Information and Application:

MCAT Program Office
P.O. Box 4056
Iowa City, IA 52243
319-337-1357

I have found that no matter how much you prepare for the MCAT you never feel completely ready for the test. All students think if they had just one more week, their studying would have been complete. Your anxiousness is normal and will help you stay focused during the test. If you think you know everything you may not concentrate as much which could lead to silly mistakes. If you have taken the time to study and follow the tips in the book, you will be ready to score well on the test.

Chapter 3

What Happens Next

After you send in your application, you will get either a rejection, a secondary application, or an interview. The time you will have to wait depends on the school you apply to. Some schools will respond in a matter of weeks. others wait till their application deadline to review all applications. If you have not received word within a short time after the schools deadline, call the administration office and ask for an update.

Rejection Letters

If you receive a rejection letter, you may want to call the school and ask to speak with an admissions officer. The admissions officer will be able to tell you why you were rejected. Sometimes he or she will take a closer look at your application and decide that you deserve a secondary application or an interview. Or maybe you were rejected for an incomplete file. The school may allow you to correct the error. You have nothing to lose after being rejected. Give the school a call.

Secondary Applications

A secondary application contains a few questions that require short essay responses. Sometimes the questions ask you to discuss controversial issues, but the goal is to evaluate your writing. For example, you may be asked how you feel about socialized medicine.

Here are a few tips:

- Make sure you understand the question.
- Ask physicians for their opinions.
- Form your own opinion, but take care not to polarize your statements.
- Above all, send them a neat and grammatically correct product.

Most schools request an application processing fee with your secondary application. If you are low on funds, request a secondary application fee waiver by calling the medical school admissions office.

Interviews

Being invited for an interview means that the school feels you are a strong candidate. Most schools have data from past years telling them how many students to invite to interviews to fill their class. For instance, to fill 100 spots, a school may interview 400 students. But do not worry about your odds. Take the approach that the interview will simply clinch their decision to offer you a spot. Here are some tips for ensuring a successful interview.

Consider the possible interview approaches

Schools use various interviewing styles. In the one-on-one approach, you are asked to interview with a couple of interviewers, one at a time. Another approach is the group interview, in which all the interviewers are in the same room asking questions. The last type is a variation on the group interview, in which the interviewers talk with you and other candidates at the same time.

Most schools use the one-on-one approach, which is a very straight forward question and answer period mixed with normal conversation. The group approach alone and with other students confuses the applicants. In the group interview, you should not dominate the conversation but should also not become a wallflower. The most successful applicants find ways to include others in the conversation. For example, if they ask you what your favorite movie is, you can tell them your choice and then ask the interviewer what his or her favorite movie is and why. Or if you are with other students, you can ask a fellow student if she has seen the movie you described and ask what she thought of the plot. Essentially, you are trying your best to have a normal conversation and trying to make people comfortable with you (a valuable skill in medicine).

Anticipate possible questions and rehearse responses

When answering an interviewer's questions, remember to think and don't react. Give thoughtful answers. Practice going through an interview. Have a friend ask you the questions such as those in the list below. Refine your answers, but do not memorize them or they will sound canned. The most frequently asked questions in medical school interviews are:

- Why do you want to be a doctor?
- What is your best quality?
- How do you deal with stress?
- Who do you rely on for support?
- How important are grades to you?
- What are your favorite hobbies?
- What is your favorite movie and why?
- If you could cure any disease, which would it be and why?
- Tell me about a life experience that made you a better person.
- What are your three greatest achievements?
- If I gave you $10,000 dollars and you could not save the money, what would you spend it on?
- What is an HMO? (See Medical Potpourri.)
- How do you feel about Universal Health Care?
- What is the difference between our health care system and Canada's?
- Where do you see yourself 10 years from now?
- Tell me about yourself.
- Why do you want to attend our school?
- How did you first become interested in medicine?
- You stated in your personal statement that.... What did you mean?
- You stated in your personal statement that.... What did you learn from that experience?
- Your professor states that you are a hard worker. What things did you do that demonstrated to your professor your diligence?

- Who is your favorite author? or What was the last book you read?
- If you don't get into medical school what would you do?
- Say you reapplied and still didn't get in what would you do?
- What if a patient asked you not to tell anyone about his disease and his wife called you to inquire about his health?
- What if the disease was transmittable to her by contact with her husband?

Interviewers ask these types of questions to see if you can think on your feet. Remember to think about your answer before responding. With all the questions, keep your answers brief and to the point.

There are no set answers for these questions. The main objective in an interview is to be enthusiastic, inoffensive, thoughtful, and conversational. Above all, have confidence in yourself: If the school thought you didn't have what it takes to become a doctor, it would not have invited you for an interview.

Dress appropriately for the interview

Men should wear a dark blue or charcoal black suit with a white shirt and conservative tie. No cartoon ties. (Don't laugh, it's been done.) You want them to remember you, not what you wore. Men should not have ponytails or earrings. It is superficial to judge people by how they wear their hair or the clothes they wear. The reason why physicians do not like applicants who deviate from the norm in appearance is because medical school requires conformity to traditions that have been passed down for many years. If you are breaking those rules before you are even accepted, that worries admissions officers. So look well groomed and conservative. You should not have any words shaved into your head. (Again, don't laugh, it has been done.) You should look well groomed.

Women should wear a professional dress or business suit. No mini-skirts, leather, or lace. No fluorescent hair colors. You may have earrings, but in no place other than your ears. And the earrings should not be extravagant. You will be walking around seeing the campus so wear comfortable shoes.

Have questions in mind to ask

Interviewers always ask if you have any questions. An interested student always has questions. If you're at all nervous, you may find it difficult to ask pertinent questions. Do not ask questions that would be better answered by a medical student. (Ask medical students about housing, financial aid, nightlife, type of curriculum, and study facilities.) Ask the interviewer about research opportunities for medical students, exposure to physician advisors, and the percentage of students who receive their first choice in the residency match. Do not ask about your chances of gaining acceptance or whether you did well in your interview.

Write the Interviewers a Thank You Letter

A thank you letter adds a professional touch and reinforces the image of the young professional. When the interviewers meet at their selection meeting, your letter may make the difference between their remembering you or not.

Write the interviewers a brief thank you letter stating how much you appreciated meeting with them. Add something in your letter about your conversation with them so that they will remember you. State that you are interested in attending their school. One paragraph is all you need.

Acceptance Letters!

First, celebrate your incredible achievement. Most schools give a deadline for you to accept their offer. It is bad form to accept an offer and then back out.

If you have other interviews, go to them. Even if you were accepted to the school of your dreams, see what the other schools have to offer. I was accepted to the school of my dreams, but I went to other interviews and discovered that another school was better for me. The school I attended offered tuition waivers for participation in research; the school of my dreams did not. The school I chose also offered more support for the student body by way of a new computer lab, student lounge, gymnasium, and monthly outings partly subsidized by the university.

The decision as to which medical school to attend is an important one. Shop around. Knowing that you have an acceptance in hand will make your other interviews easier. You will be more comfortable, and you will become aware of more questions that are pertinent to you.

How Do I Finally Choose a School?

Most physicians can tell you why they chose their medical school. The school's ranking, location, cost, social support, and research opportunities all should be high on your list. Determine the three most important criteria on your list, and make sure the school offers those things. Then consider the intangibles. For example, what's your gut feeling about the school? What was your impression of the students you met? Did they seem satisfied with the school? You are making an important decision, so take your time.

Once you make an informed decision, don't look back. You may experience times in medical school when you say, "I should have gone to School X." All students go through this, even students at School X.

Options If You're Not Accepted

As Sir Winston Churchill said, "Never, Never, Never, Never, Never, Never give up!"

First re-evaluate. If you don't receive an acceptance letter, don't despair, but take stock of where you are. First evaluate your application. If you did not receive interview invitations, maybe something in your application needs correcting. Is your MCAT score low? Consider taking a preparatory course to raise your score. Can you make the personal statement stronger? Did you get strong letters of recommendation? In college, sometimes getting to know professors well can be difficult. If you have not built a relationship with a professor, take an upper-level science course, and make a point of letting the instructor get to know you. If you can improve any part of the application process, do so and apply again.

Consider Post-baccalaureate Programs

Another option is to attend a school that offers a one-year premedical program called a post-baccalaureate program. These programs differ in the courses they offer, but most offer the same courses offered to first-year medical students. These programs require tuition payment, and some do not guarantee a spot in their upcoming class. If you consider this option, ask schools about their record of medical school placement after completing the year. Start with schools to which you have applied; if they do not offer such a program, they may be able to recommend one.

Consider Osteopathic Medicine

You may also consider going to a school of osteopathic medicine. D.O.s (Doctor of Osteopathy) complete four years of medical training followed by a one-year internship before beginning residency. Osteopathic physicians enjoy the same practice rights and privileges as M.D.s. The number of practicing D.O.s is more than 34,000. Osteopathic schools have on average an entering class of about 2,500. For more information, contact the American Association of Colleges of Osteopathic Medicine Application Service (AACOMAS).

AACOMAS
6110 Executive Blvd., Suite 405
Rockville, MD 20852-3991
301-468-2037

   or

California
College of Osteopathic Medicine of the Pacific
909-469-5335

Florida
Nova Southeastern University
305-949-4000

Illinois
Chicago College of Osteopathic Medicine of Midwestern
University
800-458-6253

Iowa
University of Osteopathic Medicine and Health Science
515-271-1578

Maine
University of New England College of Osteopathic Medicine
517-553-7140

Michigan
Michigan State University College of Osteopathic Medicine
816-626-2237

Missouri
Kinksville College of Osteopathic Medicine
816-626-2237
University of Health Science College of Osteopathic Medicine
800-234-4045

New Jersey
University of Medicine and Dentistry of New Jersey College of
Osteopathic Medicine
609-566-7050

New York
New York College of Osteopathic Medicine of the New York
Institute of Technology
516-626-6947

Ohio
Ohio University College of Osteopathic Medicine
614-593-4313

Oklahoma
Oklahoma State University College of Osteopathic Medicine
918-582-1972

Pennsylvania
Philadelphia College of Osteopathic Medicine
215-871-2711
Lake Erie College of Osteopathic Medicine
814-866-6641

Texas
Texas College of Osteopathic Medicine
817-735-2204

West Virginia
West Virginia School of Osteopathic Medicine
800-537-7077

Consider Canadian Medical Schools

Another option is medical schools in Canada approved by the Association of American Medical Colleges. The Canadian medical schools take about 10 percent of their students from outside Canada. The competition for these spots is fierce, but perhaps worth considering. The three best Canadian schools are McGill University, University of Toronto, and University of British Colombia. Three others require proficiency in French (University of Montreal, Laval, and Sherbroke). You can request admission requirements to Canadian Faculties of Medicine by sending $24 U.S. dollars to:

Association of Canadian Medical Colleges
774 Echo Drive
Ottawa, Ontario
Canada K1S 5P2

Consider Other Foreign Schools

Besides Canada, American graduates have attained acceptance to medical schools in Latin America, Spain, Italy, the Philippines, and the Caribbean. Gaining admission can be difficult for many reasons. First, you're contending with cultural and possibly language differences. Securing a residency in the U.S. is more difficult after graduating from a foreign medical school. But foreign graduates do secure residencies in the U.S. each year. Also keep in mind you must complete a residency in the U.S. to practice medicine here. For more information on foreign medical schools, call the consulate of the country whose schools you are considering.

Preparing for Medical School after Acceptance

Some medical students say you should do nothing but enjoy yourself before school starts. I agree to some extent, but you can do a few things to help yourself.

You may not have had any exposure to medical school classes. In your first year of medical school, you will be responsible for gross anatomy, histology, biochemistry, neuroanatomy, physiology, behavioral science, and genetics. (For more information on medical school courses, see Chapter 4.) If you have not had anatomy, I suggest you buy the Atlas of Human Anatomy by Frank Netter. In medical school, you will be learning a new language, and that language begins with anatomy. Look at the pictures and familiarize yourself with the vocabulary.

Also, talk to physicians and let them know that you will be starting medical school. Ask them if you can follow them for a few days. Pick physicians who are in specialties that you are considering. If you do not have a specialty in mind, observe one nonsurgical and one surgical physician. Purchase a medical dictionary and look up words that come up during your observations.

Make sure that you have moved into your new residence a few weeks before the first day of school. You want no external stresses besides school when you start. Also, during those weeks, get to know your surroundings.

Lastly, if you are not familiar with computers, take the summer before medical school to gain a working knowledge of computers. Computers are being used more and more in medicine. Doctors use the computer to locate research articles, develop slides for presentations, and access the Internet for information. I've listed a few medical web sites below, and you can find others in Appendix 1.

http:www-med.stanford.edu/MedSchool/MedWorld/lounge-links.html#search

http://www.pslgroup.com/medsites.htm
"Doctor's Guide to the Web"

http://medicus.marshall.edu/medicus.htm
"The interactive patient"

Below is a checklist of deadlines that you should be aware of during college. If you follow the schedule below you will have your applications in on time which will give you an advantage when applying because admissions are based on rolling admissions. (Rolling admissions policy means the school considers each application as it comes in from AMCAS or from the individual. Once their incoming class is filled, they stop interviewing and accepting students.) If a school does not have a rolling admissions policy, then they have an applications deadline.

PRE-MED CHECKLIST AND CALENDAR

FRESHMAN AND SOPHOMORE YEAR
Volunteer at local hospital
Check Appendix 1 for each medical school's requirements
Take summer courses to lighten course load for junior year

JUNIOR YEAR
Before January
Letters of recommendation
Complete personal statement
Request AMCAS application
Complete study schedule for April MCAT

April
Take April MCAT exam
After exam, complete AMCAS

June 15
Earliest day to submit AMCAS

August 1
Last day to submit AMCAS for EDP
Schools have deadlines for applications ranging
from October 15 to December 15.
Mail your applications by August 15 to give AMCAS
at least two months to process your application.

SENIOR YEAR
September
MCAT retake if needed
Med school in one year

November
Secondary applications and interviews begin this month
Process can go on until April

September
Med school begins

If you have followed the advice given, you have increased your chances of getting into medical school. The remaining sections in this book will be a medical student's survival guide. Take a deep breath, roll up your sleeves, get the coffee maker going because now the real hard part starts.

*Chapter 4*_____

Medical School: The First Two Years

Medical school does not build character but reveals it.
—*Anonymous*

In medical school you are known as an M1, M2, M3, or M4. The divisions correspond to the years you are in school. In the next three chapters, I will explain what to expect, how to succeed, and how to plan for each year in the medical school process.

In general, the first two years are known as the basic science years. The subjects in the first year include gross anatomy, histology, neuroanatomy, embryology, behavioral science, physiology, and biochemistry. In the second year, you'll cover microbiology, pathology, pharmacology, physical diagnosis, and more behavioral science. Both the traditional and new curricula are outlined in this chapter

"Boards"

No matter what curriculum your school follows, you will be responsible for passing the United States Medical Licensure Exam (USMLE), a.k.a. "Boards." You have three Boards exams. First, most students take USMLE 1 after their second year. It covers the basic sciences. You'll take USMLE 2 after the M3 year and USMLE 3 during your internship. Both test your clinical knowledge. More on Boards later.

In the third and fourth year, you will do rotations in the hospital. Most students are required to complete rotations in internal medicine, obstetrics and gynecology, pediatrics, surgery, psychiatry, and others. After the required rotations, you select elective rotations. Some of these include plastic surgery, dermatology, ophthalmology, and cardiology.

Goals for Medical School

Most schools will tell you that they do not have a competitive atmosphere at their school to foster more camaraderie. Well do not believe them because even if the school does not give grades or rank their students your national boards scores will help residencies rank you. Also, the same competitive people who you met in undergraduate college are now in medical school. So, before starting your first year assess what you want from your four years of medical school. If you are like most students, you want to be an above-average medical student: Good students gain good residencies.

Some specialties are so competitive that average to below-average students can have a hard time gaining a place in the specialty of their choice. Some students think that if they are going for a noncompetitive specialty, they don't have to excel in medical school. But sometimes these students change their minds and go after competitive positions. Unfortunately, after three years of sub-par performance, they find it hard to gain a residency. Even if you are going for a noncompetitive specialty, keep your grades up for the best choice of residency programs.

The bottom line is to do your best and strive to be an excellent student. You should not become a competitive jerk, a.k.a. a "gunner," but never forget that a medical school degree alone does not guarantee a good residency.

Residency programs use many criteria to choose residents, including class ranking, letters of recommendation, participation in extracurricular activities, and Boards scores. Strive to excel in these areas, especially with 1) your scores on USMLE 1, 2) your letters of recommendation, and 3) if you want to gain acceptance in an academic residency, research.

The First Year (M1)

There are many things you can do as an M1. You can join student government, begin research, join medical societies, volunteer for community help groups, and party with new friends. I forgot to mention your classes, where you will be expected to learn tons of information in a short time. Before you spread yourself too thin, know that your main job in medical school is to learn as much as possible. In each passing year, you will have less and less time to read medical texts. Take advantage of the time you have now to read.

You will be required to attend lectures each day, except on weekends, and attend labs a few times a week. The labs will be for gross anatomy, where you will dissect cadavers. You will also have labs in histology, where you will look at microscopic slides of sections of the human body.

You will quickly learn that if you attend all these classes you will be spending most of your days listening and not studying. You'll need to make some choices. People in education know that there are many educational modalities that can be used to teach. Lecturing is one of these modalities, but not all students learn best through lecturing. Some students learn better by other means, such as reading text, creating graphs and pictures, writing, studying in small groups, and working one on one with other students.

Here are some general tips to maximize the time you spend studying and in lectures.

Lectures

"The lecture is the most inefficient method of diffusing culture. It became obsolete with the invention of printing. It survives only in our universities and their lay imitators, and a few other backward institutions..... Why don't you just hand print lectures to your students? Yes, I know. Because they won't read them. A fine institution it is that must solve that problem with platform chicanery" (B.F. Skinner, Walden 2 1948).

I don't fully agree with Skinner's interpretation of lectures. They do have their place but you should be prepared for the lecture, and the educator must be good. Most students feel bad if they miss lecture. Don't worry: Most schools have a student-run note-taking system. Students take turns attending lectures and writing notes for that lecture. If you do not attend a lecture, use that time to study. If you attend a lecture, be adequately prepared. Study the topic to be covered the night before, taking outlined notes. While in the lecture, supplement your notes with information from the lecturer. Do not vegetate in lecture. If you find yourself staring at the wall, leave, grab yourself some coffee, and study on your own.

Study Guides

Use your lecture notes and Boards review books to study. You will be using these books for Boards review, so buy them now, and become familiar with them. When you begin studying for Boards, you will be able to review the books instead of reading them for the first time just months before the exam.

Along with review books, I recommend using question books for each subject. Two books that I recommend have book lists that tell you which are the best books for your classes and also provide USMLE 1 tips. They are *The Medical Student's Guide to Top Board Scores*, by

P. Thomas Rodgers and *First Aid for the Boards,* by Vikas Bhushan and Jeffrey Hansen.

Memory Techniques

Because you have so much information to learn in a short amount of time, use memory techniques. Here are some techniques and examples.

Mnemonics

Mnemonics are techniques used to assist memory. They can take many forms. One example of a mnemonic is an easy-to-remember word made from the first letters of a list of items. Try to find a word that gives you an image in your mind that links to the information you want to memorize.

For example, you may want to memorize all the infections that cause failure to thrive when passed from mother to baby in the womb or during birth. Picture a mother passing the TORCH to her child.

T - toxoplasmosis
O - other - like syphilis
R - rubella
C - CMV
H - herpes

Keep the mnemonic simple; don't make remembering the mnemonic more difficult than remembering the information.

Here's another example. The bacteria Staphylococcus Aureus causes STAPHEO.

S - skin infections, scalded skin syndrome
T - toxic shock syndrome
A - abscesses
P - pneumonia
H - hemolysis (beta)
E - endocarditis
O - osteomyeolitis

You can also use a funny sentence to remember the letters and order of certain information. Do not use full sentences too often because they take more time to create and often don't work as well for long-term memory.

Here's an example. For the branches of the axillary artery in order, you might use the sentence "Sally Thompson loves sex and pot": Supreme Thoracic, Thoracoacromial, Lateral thoracic, Subscapular, Anterior circumflex, Posterior circumflex.

You can also develop analogies in the form of images to help you memorize information. At the scapular notch there is a transverse scapular ligament that has an artery (suprascapular) that runs over it and a nerve (suprascapular) running under it. A professor told me to think of the ligament as a bridge; the army goes on top of the bridge, and the navy uses the water under the bridge. Army - Artery and Navy- Nerve.

Mnemonics are best when you think of them yourself. If you make a word out of information, the word should conjure up an image meaningful to you. The theory is that you are connecting new information to information you already have in your mind. Recall becomes easier and permanent.

And use other techniques to help you remember information: tables, pictures, and flow charts.

Study Groups

The study strategies mentioned above are ones you primarily use alone. But some students learn better in groups. The information becomes fixed in their minds when they explain it to their peers. If you prefer this type of learning, set up study groups. Study groups require patience by all involved because covering all of the material takes more time than studying alone.

In gross anatomy you will be placed in groups for cadaver dissection. The anatomy group can also function as a study group. Divide the work evenly. Make sure one person in the group prepares intensely for the dissection of that day. Have the leader for that day teach the rest of the group.

Use a similar technique for study groups. Have each person study a particular topic thoroughly, but all of you study each topic also. Then each person presents his or her topic. Ask questions of each other. When explaining information, have your reference book close at hand. When your group members are unclear about a certain point, they may go over your reference. Also, if you do not fully know the answer to a question, say, "I do not know the answer. Let's look it up." Not knowing something is better than giving misinformation.

Try all the study methods; see which ones work best for you. Then use them.

Formal Review Sessions

Attend, tape record, and take good notes of all formal review sessions. Professors use review sessions to tell you what they think are the most important points you should have learned from their classes. If you record the lecture, you can go over each point they made in depth.

Also, just as you may have done in college, try to find old exams to figure out exam patterns and topics about which professors seem to test.

Shadowing Physicians

Before you started medical school, you followed physicians to gain a clearer perspective of medicine as a career. Continue to follow physicians, and choose ones in different specialties. The day when you have to decide your specialty comes more quickly than you expect. If you shadow physicians now, you will have a better idea of the specialties you are considering. Also, as a bystander you will get a different perspective on a specialty than you will as a third- or fourth-year medical student. As an M3 and M4, you are expected to work, not observe in a relaxed setting.

Shadowing also reminds you why you chose to be a doctor. As an M1 and M2, learning the basic sciences with minimal patient contact, you may forget that your ultimate goal is caring for people. Most schools are trying to remedy the gap between lack of patient contact and the first two years. But even with the changes, many medical students find it difficult to pick a residency. Take the time to look firsthand at the different specialties early in medical school; making a career choice will be easier.

Extracurricular Activities

Although participating in extracurricular activities will help make you stand out, don't jump to join these activities until you see how you handle the normal workload. To help give you an idea of how best to spend your time, here's a rundown of how each activity will demand your time and how to best handle the extra work.

Student Government. Serving in student government can be a rewarding job. Each school has a student council with elected officials from the student body. The council usually meets once or twice a month to discuss and vote on school policies. As a student council representative, you are responsible for being the students' advocate. Other responsibilities include organizing social gatherings, distributing information from the Dean's Office of Student Affairs to the student body, and helping the Dean's Office with school activities. For example, when prospective students visit the school for interviews, you will be asked to show them the school. Serving in student government consumes study time but you are truly serving the school and your classmates. If you are interested in school politics this will be a good outlet for your energy. Some residencies like students who have participated in student government because it shows a commitment to making your immediate environment better. They assume you will show the same level of commitment during residency.

Research. Research will benefit you in many ways such as teaching you analytical thinking, applying for grants, presenting scientific material, and most of all, patience when things don't go your way. You could also make a significant contribution to medicine. If you don't believe me, there is the Banting and Best story.

In 1923, Sir Frederick Grant Banting, a surgeon and physiologist, won a Nobel Prize for isolating and purifying insulin as the substance secreted by the pancreas to regulate blood sugar. He completed the research with the help of a medical student named Charles H. Best. Sir Banting, on accepting the award, recognized Best and divided his share of the prize with him. Today in Ontario there is The Banting and Best Department of Medical Research.

The Banting and Best story demonstrates the ultimate pinnacle a medical student can reach. The worst case scenario is the Bury and Burn story. A student named Burn went to Dr. Bury for a research position. Burn did not ask about his role in the research project. He assumed that he would be an integral part of the study and had visions of being the next Charles Best. In two years, his role in the project never exceeded the feeding of the rats used for the project. Feeding rats or cleaning test tubes will not help you learn about research.

Maximize the benefit of your research experience before you begin work. Ask many questions before joining a project: What will be my role in the project? Will I be involved in literature searches, writing research protocols, applying for grants, performing the experiments, and presenting results at meetings? Will I be meeting with you once a week to discuss the progress of the project? Can I receive a tuition waiver or stipend for my work? Can I use grant money as salary? Will I be able to complete this project before I start my third year? (You will not have flexible hours to do research during your clinical M3 and M4 years.)

These questions will help make your objectives clear and allow you to choose the right situation for your ultimate goals. And talk with students who have worked with the researcher about their experiences.

There are two types of research: clinical and laboratory. Clinical research involves interviewing patients, reviewing medical records, administering drug trials, and anything that does not require laboratory benchwork. Laboratory research involves the use of animals or investigations requiring lab benchwork. Usually clinical research requires less time and work than laboratory projects. Some lab researchers spend years on one project. As a medical student, you do not have years to spend on a project. Most students who complete research average 15 hours a week during the school year and work full time during the summer. (After the M1 year you have summer vacation lasting close to three months.) Most residencies do not care what type of research you chose, clinical or laboratory. Residency programs look for publication or presentation of your research and the extent of your involvement in the project.

If you want to devote even more time to research, you have many options. Most schools will allow you to take a year off between your second and third years to complete research. The National Institutes of Health have the Howard Hughes Medical Institute, which offers research training fellowships for medical students. For more information, you can reach them at:

Hughes Fellowship Program
The Fellowship Office
National Research Council
2101 Constitution Avenue
Washington, DC 20418
202-334-3419

Community Outreach

You might also consider community outreach.

"Sometimes give your services for nothing, calling to mind a previous benefaction or present satisfaction. .... For where there is love of man, there is also love of the art. For some patients, though conscious that their condition is perilous, recover their health simply through their contentment with the goodness of the physician" (Hippocrates 460-400 B.C.).

Some of my most memorable moments in medical school are the times I spent volunteering in community outreach programs. The programs included activities such as lecturing to high school students on the dangers of drugs or AIDS. Also, while volunteering at health fairs, I performed free physical examinations for the poor. And once I helped collect used toys to be donated to our hospital's pediatrics ward. The same year we collected canned foods for donation to the local homeless shelters. If your school does not have these programs in place, begin them yourself. These projects were all initially started by students. The time spent is well worth the trouble.

A Final Word about the First Year

Early in your first year, talk with as many upperclassmen as possible about the school's curriculum. Ask them how the exams are and how best to study for them. Ask about the quality of instruction in the various classes. There may be some lecturers you will not want to miss. Try to acquire old notes and exams. Since upperclassmen have already been through the system, they are a valuable resource.

After the first year, you have the summer off. Use the time wisely. Focus on research, study for the following year, follow physicians, and start to think about what specialty appeals to you. You can acquire more information on the various specialties from their respective associations. (See Appendix 2.) Also, recharge for the coming year because everything from this point on will come at a quicker pace.

The Second Year (M2)

In the second year, you will be responsible for pathology, microbiology, pharmacology, introduction to physical diagnosis, more behavioral science and USMLE Part 1. In this year you will begin to bridge the gap between basic science and clinical medicine.

By this time you will already have developed your study strategies. Use the strategies that have been working for you, but do not be afraid to try new ones. You should expect even more memorization and less abstract thinking in this year.

You may want to try group question-and-answer periods. In a group of at least five, assign each student to write 10 questions and answers for a particular subject. Then take turns covering questions and answers. Liven things up by making a competition out of the sessions. These sessions will prepare you for the hospital floors, where physicians will be putting you on the spot to answer questions (a.k.a. "pimping").

The Hospital Hierarchy

During your physical diagnosis class, you will have your first real exposure to the hospital and its hierarchy. The top of the hierarchy begins with the Chief of the Department, followed by attending physicians, chief resident, residents, interns, M4s, and M3s in that order. The chief runs the department and oversees the other physicians in the department. Attending physicians have worked in the department, finished their residencies, and have hospital privileges. The chief resident recently finished his residency and now completes the day-to-day administrative chores. Interns are first-year residents just recently graduated from medical school. The other residents have completed their first year of residency and they oversee the intern.

A team usually consists of an attending, a few residents in different years in their residencies, a few interns, some third-, and possibly some fourth-year medical students. During the second year, you will have only a glance at how a team works. Your main objective in physical diagnosis class is to learn how to complete a medical history and physical exam.

Completing a Medical History

I have an easy format to help you conduct and write a thorough history and physical. Also, this presentation method will earn you high marks on your rotations. First, use the CHAMP FASTS mnemonic to remember the order of questions you should ask during each history.

Below are the CHAMP FASTS steps and a brief description of each step.

C - Chief Complaint (CC) - includes a brief explanation as to why the patient has come to the hospital and how long the patient has had the problem.

Example:
CC - Chest Pain of 1-hour duration five hours ago

H - History of Present Illness (HPI) - includes all information pertinent to the patient's Chief Complaint. Include risk factors, active diseases pertinent to the current problem, and the progression of the disease, all in chronological order. When describing any type of pain, always ask the pertinent questions covered by the mnemonic COLDERRA. (See next paragraph.) Also, include any pertinent negative symptomological findings relevant to a suspected disease. Always end your HPI with an administrative sentence stating why the patient was admitted to the hospital.

Mnemonic for questions to be asked of patient's pain. COLDERRA
C - characteristics of pain
O - onset
L - location
D - duration
E - exacerbation
R - relief
R - radiation
A - associated symptoms

Example:
HPI - Patient is a 55-year-old white male admitted and diagnosed with a myocardial infarction one year ago. At that time, it was determined through angiogram that he had 20 percent blockage of the left anterior descending artery. The etiology of his coronary artery disease

is a 40-year smoking history of at least one pack a day and hypertension of 20 years. He has been taking Propranolol and aspirin since the admission one year ago. Pt. states he has been compliant with his medications. Pt. had no further problems until two days prior to admission. Pt. complained of a substernal chest pain of 1-hr. duration, which began when he was moving some heavy boxes at work. The pain was unrelieved by rest or by taking sublingual nitrogen given to him by the company nurse. Pt. states that the pain feels like pressure much like the sensation he felt with his heart attack a year ago. Pt. states that the pain radiates to his left shoulder but not to his jaw. Pt. did not complain of diaphoresis, nausea, dizziness, weakness, vomiting or loss of consciousness. Pt. is being admitted for his chest pain and to rule out a myocardial infarction.

A - Allergies - Include any drug allergies and even significant non-drug allergies.

Example:
Allergies - Penicillin and Hayfever

M - Medications - Include all the medications, with dosing regime, that the person was taking before admission. Include even minor medications such as aspirin. If the patient must have an emergency surgical procedure, the surgeon will want to know if the patient has taken even aspirin.

Example:
Meds - Propranolol 120mg three times a day
       Aspirin 325mg once a day

P - Past Medical History and Past Surgical History (PMH and PSH) - Include all significant history: include all surgeries and any medical condition that required a doctor's care excluding minor infections, bronchitis, etc. Include dates if possible.

Example:
PMH - MI last year, HTN discovered last year
PSH - Right tibia fracture externally fixated in 1982,
       Appendectomy 35 yrs. ago

F - Family History (FH) - Include all familial (genetic) risk factors. For example, any disease that has a genetic basis - breast cancer, diabetes, myocardial infarction, manic-depression. Histories of relatives not related genetically should not be included.

Example:

FH - Younger brother died of a heart attack last year. Father and grandfather both died of heart attacks before the age of 60. Mother had hypertension.

A - Alcohol - Include the amount per day. If pt. states he is a social drinker, clarify his definition of a social drinker. You must obtain a quantifiable answer.

Example:

A - 3 beers a week, 2 cups of whiskey once a month

S - Street Drugs - Include any illegal drug use including abuse of prescription drugs.

Example:

S - Marijuana twice a month

T - Tobacco - Do not use "pack years," which is the number of packs per day per year. This can be a misleading number and will not tell you if the patient has quit and for how many years.

Example:

T - 1 pack a day for 40 yrs. but quit one month ago.

S - Social History - Include work history, diet, sexual history, family in the area, and psychological stressors. Stressors include a death in the family, divorce, unemployment, sick child, etc.

Example:

S - Pt. works at the Banks Co. loading dock. He has been there for 20 years as a shipping clerk. He states that he usually eats eggs and toast in the morning, a ham sandwich for lunch, and usually meat and potatoes for dinner. He is recently divorced and lives alone. He has three children who all live in the city.

The history mnemonic does not include Review of Systems (ROS). After completing CHAMPS FASTS you have one more step before starting your physical examination - Review of Systems (ROS).

ROS - Include any medical problems other than the ones described in the HPI. Most of the time these will include problems that are noncontributory to the current disease process. Begin your questioning with the head, and continue down until you reach the toes.

ROS - Pain in the left knee

The CHAMP FASTS plus ROS mnemonic will allow you to conduct your history in a consistent and systematic manner. You will not omit pertinent information from your history.

Completing a Physical Exam

After the history, follow with the physical examination. The write-up should begin with the patient's vital signs and then general appearance.

Vital Signs - Include blood pressure, pulse, temperature, and respiration rate.

General Appearance - Describe what the patient looks like and his or her general condition. Patient appears pale and anxious but in no apparent distress.

The physical exam (PE) is a straightforward process. Your physical diagnosis class will cover the details. Complete the write-up as follows.

- Head, eyes, ears, nose, throat (Use the mnemonic HEENT.)
- Lungs
- Cardiovascular - include heart and pulses
- Abdomen
- Rectum and genitalia - include rectal exam
- Extremities
- Neurological
- Skin
- Mental status
- Breast and pelvic

After documenting these parts of the exam, include all the studies. Use the mnemonic CUBS for the order:

C - complete blood count (CBC). Always include results of all blood work: hemoglobin, hematocrit, white blood cell count, platelets and a differential if one is included. Most people use a diagram like the one below to show the CBC with differential.

U - urinalysis.

B - blood studies. Include results of all blood studies: BUN, creatinine, electrolytes, ABG, chemistry, coagulation studies, toxicology, cardiac enzymes, etc. A simple shorthand method for documenting BUN, creatinine, and lytes results is shown below.

S - special studies. Include the results of any special studies: chest X-ray, echocardiogram, CT scan, MRI, EKG, etc.

Assessing the Patient and Planning Treatment

Now you are ready for the assessment and treatment plan. The most straightforward way to accomplish this is to list each problem with the assessment and plan following.

Example:

1. Rule Out MI - Patient has elevated cardiac enzymes. Pt. also has inverted T-waves on EKG. These studies, with the past history of MI, point to another myocardial infarction. Will schedule echocardiogram, angiogram, and repeat EKG to document extent of disease. Will continue telemetry bed, oxygen, propranolol, and aspirin. Wait for test results. Continue present management.
2. Painful Tender Knee - No apparent acute injury; most likely osteo-arthritic changes. May give ibuprofen for pain. Continue to monitor.

Presenting the Patient to Your Team

You will be called upon to present your patients to your team everyday. The presentations are called rounds. Rounds can be conducted in a conference room or at the bedside of each patient. Rounds are conducted in the morning after all the patients have been seen individually by the person responsible for the individual patient. Usually, as a student, you are responsible for one to five patients sometimes more depending how busy your team is at the time. Most of the time, you only have a few minutes to prepare so I will give you a blueprint how to present so you can quickly prepare an excellent presentation every time.

When you present a patient to interns, residents, and attendings, the key is to give all the pertinent information in three to five minutes. The format for presentation differs slightly from that of your write-up. Begin with the patient's name, and state the chief complaint exactly as in the write-up. Your HPI will also be exactly the same. Be sure to include in chronological order all pertinent information including current medications, risk factors for current illness, and active diseases pertinent to the case.

If allergies, medications, PMH, PSH, "FASTS," and ROS are contributory, include them in the HPI. If they are not, state that these are non-contributory or otherwise covered in the HPI. This statement tells your audience that you are ready to move on to the physical exam (PE).

When presenting your findings from the physical exam, always start with vital signs and general appearance. Then give pertinent positive and pertinent negative findings. For example, say you are considering a fracture in a patient, and he or she does not have point tenderness at the sight of suspected fracture. The lack of point tenderness would be a pertinent negative.

Then give the studies in the CUBS format. If any imaging studies have been done, have them on the view box ready to show. Follow the studies with the assessment and treatment plan.

Example of a Presentation:

Mr. Halsted has a chief complaint of chest pain of one-hour duration.

Patient is a 55-year-old white male who was admitted and diagnosed with a myocardial infarction one year ago. At that time it was determined through angiogram that he had 20 percent blockage of the left anterior descending artery. The etiology of his coronary artery disease is a 40-year smoking history of at least one pack a day and hypertension of twenty years. He has been taking Propranolol and aspirin since the admission of one year ago. Pt. states he has been compliant with his medications.

Pt. had no further problems until the day of admission. Pt. complained of a substernal chest pain of 1-hr. duration, which began when he was moving some heavy boxes at work. The pain was unrelieved by rest or by taking sublingual nitrogen given to him by the company nurse. Pt. was brought in by a company worker three hours later. Pt. on admission stated that the pain feels like pressure much like the sensation he felt when he had his heart attack a year ago. Pt. states that the pain radiates to his left shoulder but not to his jaw. Pt. did not complain of diaphoresis, nausea, dizziness, weakness, vomiting, or loss of consciousness. Pt. is being admitted for his chest pain and to rule out a myocardial infarction.

All other history, including other active diseases and ROS, are noncontributory or otherwise covered in the HPI. Pt. was afebrile, with a blood pressure of 140 over 90, pulse of 80, and respiration rate of 18. Pt. was pale but alert, responsive, and in no apparent distress. Physical exam was significant for tenderness in the left shoulder. Pt. has a cardiac gallop rhythm. No pulmonary rales or jugular venous distention. No other significant physical findings. Pt.'s CBC had a normal hemoglobin, hematocrit, platelets with a slightly elevated WBC of 14.2 with a normal differential. No UA was obtained. BUN, creatinine and lytes were all normal. Pt. had a normal CPK on admission with an abnormal increase to 222, 6 hrs. later. Pt. had a abnormal LDH ratio 24 hrs. after admission. LDH 1 was higher than LDH 2. Pt. had an abnormal ECG with elevated ST segments. Chest X-ray was normal. No other studies have been completed.

This patient is a 55-yr. old male who has just suffered his second episode of myocardial infarction. Pt. was placed on nitroglycerin, procainamide, and morphine sulfate acutely. We will continue his current medications of Propranolol and aspirin. Pt. is scheduled for an echocardiogram and angiogram to check ejection fraction and extent of coronary disease respectively.

With this format you can deliver your presentation in less than five minutes without leaving out any relevant information. After the presentation, the attending will begin to ask you questions about the case. Know your patient and anticipate the questions. Also, make sure you've completed a literature search on your patient's disease. You will be able to teach your team current information on diagnosis and management. The attending will be impressed, and you will be rendering good care to your patient.

After the presentation, keep good track of the patient's progress. Attendings will sometimes ask how your patient is progressing, and if you don't know, all your work during the presentation will be for naught. Enjoy these presentations because you will be giving them for at least the next six years.

Note: I suggest you write the presentations on 3 x 5 index cards, and try to memorize them. If you cannot run through the presentation smoothly without the cards, use them. Also, always go through your presentation ahead of time with a doctor on your team. If the doctors don't have time to listen to your presentation, practice with one of your classmates.

USMLE 1

The USMLE 1 is a two-day multiple choice exam offered in June and September. Most students take the June test, but some students take it in September. Some students believe a delay in taking the test will give them more months to study. I believe it instead allows you more time to forget information.

Most students do not ever feel ready to take the exam. The amount of information you are responsible for is more than you will ever retain. If you've been studying well all along, three months of extra preparation will not help you. If you've followed my earlier advice, you are already familiar with the various review books and the most helpful USMLE 1 study books. Review these. Feel confident about your preparation. Then struggle through the two-day exam like every medical student before you.

After USMLE 1, you will begin rotations, which marks the beginning of the third year.

Once you have completed the test, you will be entering the hospital full time and beginning patient care. Some students have problems making the transition from classroom student to the world of hands-on medicine in the hospital. The following sections in the book will tell you what to expect on the hospital floors and should ease your anxiousness about working in the hospital.

Chapter 5

The Third Year

*"A person of very moderate ability may be a good physician,
if he devotes himself faithfully to the work."*
— *Oliver Wendell Holmes*

In the third year you will be responsible for the core clerkships. A clerkship is the time spent learning one specialty in medicine. The core clerkships are the clerkships that every medical student in the country must complete in medical school to be licensed to practice medicine. These clerkships include internal medicine, surgery, psychiatry, obstetrics and gynecology, and pediatrics. In this chapter, I will cover each core clerkship, describing your responsibilities and strategies so you may excel in the rotation.

During your fourth year, you will be applying for residency. To secure a good residency in the specialty of your choice, you must excel in the third year of medical school. Your performance depends on your evaluations from the attending physicians. Your interaction with attendings will be brief, but you must make the most of these opportunities.

A good evaluation depends not only on your performance, but also on the quality of your interactions with your team members. You will be working mostly with the residents and interns. Their letters of evaluation and letters of recommendation mean nothing, but they can influence the attendings' evaluations, so treat them with the respect their position deserves. The advice that holds true in each rotation is to know your place and know your patients.

When I say know your place, I am not suggesting that you be meek, but that you realize that, as a third year, you have very little clinical experience. Be ready to answer questions you're asked, but don't make the mistake of correcting other team members in front of the team. If you know someone in the team is wrong about something, pull him or her aside later and ask for more information. You may find that you were wrong. If you were right, the team member will appreciate your question or help.

Don't commit political suicide by making enemies. The time to show off your knowledge is during the presentations of your patients. If you know your patients to the point that you are not creating extra work for the intern and resident, you are doing an excellent job. As an attending once told me, "Show me a medical student that only triples my work, and you will be showing me an excellent student."

After each clerkship, you will be tested on the material presented in that clerkship. These exam scores will be added to your evaluations. The exam will comprise a small percentage of your overall evaluation, but it sometimes can make a difference between an excellent and an above average score.

During your clerkship you not only must stay abreast of your patients, but also read enough to do well on the exam. Buy a review book for each clerkship. For each core clerkship I will give you a few recommended texts. But the best way to find out which books are the best for the clerkships is to ask your upper classmen because there is usually a consensus on which books are the best. Do not buy a regular text because you will not be able to finish it before the clerkship exam.

Along with the review book, construct your own review sheets. The review sheets should be concise notes that are formatted in a way for quick review. For example, you can write down a heading of a disease then the three most important characteristics of the disease and then one line for a question that is typically asked about the disease. The question can be from a review book or a question by an attending on rounds. After the exam add material covered on the test but not in your review sheets. Also, before each exam purchase a USMLE 2 question book, and complete the questions relevant to each clerkship. These strategies will prepare you for both your clerkship exams and the USMLE 2.

Similar to the USMLE 1, USMLE 2 is a two-day multiple choice exam. But this exam will test you on the clinical core clerkships: pediatrics, internal medicine, preventative medicine and public health, obstetrics and gynecology, psychiatry, and surgery.

The Internal Medicine Core Clerkship

Internal Medicine is the cornerstone of any specialty that you may choose. In this clerkship, you will be learning the basic principles of patient examination, impression, and treatment. You will use these skills everyday for the rest of your life. When you are on this clerkship just tell your family and friends that you won't be around much. You will be in the hospital all day and when not on the floors, you should be in the library studying. If you work hard and learn much during this clerkship, your other clerkships will be easier because information that is presented in Internal Medicine presents itself in the other specialties.

What happens in a normal day of Internal Medicine?

During pre-rounds, interns, residents, and medical students go to the hospital and see their individual patients. During the pre-rounds you will check all of your patients' new labs. You will see your patients and ask them about any new problems or any changes in their past problems. Pre-rounds are conducted everyday.

You will also be responsible for acquiring any new film studies from the radiology department. If you have time, you can complete the notes on each patient. Each day a note must be written on each of your patients. So if you do not complete them after each pre-round, you will have to complete them later.

After each pre-round, you will meet with the most senior resident and discuss your patients. You will not be giving a formal presentation; you'll briefly run down any changes in each patient's condition, test results, your assessments and treatment plans.

Then you will meet for rounds with the attending physician. These rounds happen each day so that the attending physician will know what is happening with his patients who are in the hospital. During these rounds you will formally present your new patients and give updates on patients that you have previously presented who are still in the hospital. It is during rounds when you will use the format explained in "Presenting the Patient to Your Team" section. These rounds will be conducted at the bedside or in a conference room.

Bedside rounds are conducted with the whole team in front of the patient in their room. You will be presenting the patient as the team stands around the bed and listens. If there are any sensitive issues concerning the patient, make the attending and team aware of them before the presentation. For example, if the patient exhibits paranoid behavior, the attending might not want the whole team in the room so the patient will not be made uncomfortable.

The rest of the day is spent attending to your patients and their studies, admitting new patients, attending internal medicine lectures, and completing hospital notes on each patient (described in more detail below). To remember all your duties for the day, make a list. You will hear your list referred to as "scut list" by your team members. (Scut refers to all the work that does not require much intellectual capacity but requires much time and energy. For example, drawing blood, taking a patient to radiology and X-ray, picking up X-rays, debriding wounds, taking blood pressure, etc.)

How do I write a note?

Most hospitals use the SOAP mnemonic format for note-writing.

S - Subjective. How does the patient feel? You will record basically what the patient states.

Example:

S - Patient states that she had some headaches last night, but she feels her abdominal pain is decreasing, and she is hungry. No diarrhea since yesterday.

O - Objective. The objective section includes, in order, vital signs, overall appearance, physical exam findings, and new lab results in the CUBS format. Conduct a thorough physical exam, but keep the write-up brief and to the point.

O - BP 120/80 Pulse 80 Respiration Rate 14 Temp. 98.6
Pt. appears comfortable and in no apparent distress.
*HEENT - pupils reactive, sclera clear, mucosa moist, no lymphadenopathy
*Lungs - clear to auscultation
*Abdomen - decreased tenderness in the right lower quadrant, positive bowel sounds, no rebound tenderness, no shifting dullness, no masses felt
*Extremities - negative psoas sign,
*Rectal - no tenderness, heme negative
*Pelvic - done last night, no positive signs
*Other exam - unremarkable
Pelvic ultrasound - Negative
KUB X-ray - no specific pathological findings

A and P - Assessment and Plan. These go hand in hand. We covered these in the last chapter.

Example:

A/P -
1. Rule out appendicitis - No fever, leukocytosis, psoas sign with improving abdominal tenderness and increased appetite. Patient probably does not have appendicitis, but will observe for the rest of the day.
2. Rule out pelvic masses - Pelvic exam, ultrasound, and KUB all are negative. Probably does not have a mass. Ob/Gyn will be called on consult for another pelvic exam.

3. Initial abdominal pain - No elevation in liver or pancreas enzymes, so not likely pancreatitis or cholecystitis. Pt. probably had an acute infectious process. Wait for results of new pelvic exam. Start on liquid diet, and progress to solid diet. If pt. continues to improve and can tolerate feedings, will discharge tomorrow.

How much responsibility for patients will I have as a medical student?

During the clinical years you are responsible for your patients, but the ultimate responsibility falls on your intern, resident, and attending. Since you do not have the ultimate responsibility, any procedure or medication given to the patient must be cleared by your supervising physician. Even your notes will be countersigned by a doctor.

Although you must work with supervision, act independently to demonstrate to your intern that you know your patient. For example, sometimes patients need prescriptions for their medications. You do not have the authority to prescribe drugs, but you can write the prescription and have it ready for the intern to check and sign. (See below for the way to write a prescription.) Completing small duties like these will make you a valuable member of the team, serve as good practice, and lead to an outstanding evaluation.

Drug prescriptions

You will not have the authority to prescribe medications, but you should learn how to write prescriptions during your third year. Your intern will ask you to write out prescriptions for her so that she can just sign them and give the prescription to the patient. If you know how to write a prescription you will become more valuable to the team.

Drug Name (Generic name unless otherwise specified) Dose (mg, ml, etc.)

#Quantity - how many pills total in the bottle

# of tablets - route of administration - how often

T = 1tablet, TT = 2tablets

PO = per oral, PR = per rectum

Q = how often - i.e. Q6hrs = every six hours

Special Instructions: Take only for pain or fever; take for two days and stop.

PRN = take this medication (e.g., PRN for fever).

Example:
Ibuprofen 600mg
#25 tablets
T PO Q6hrs PRN for pain

What should I learn during my rotation?

During your internal medicine rotation, you should learn medicine, presenting during rounds, interpreting lab values, and dealing with patients and your team. These are the obvious skills you will learn during your rotation. But don't overlook the more basic skills: starting an intravenous line (IV), performing a lumbar puncture (LP), taking arterial blood gas (ABG), placing a Foley catheter and a nasogastric tube, and performing other procedures. Many med students call these procedures scut. You will never hear people say the word happily. Sometimes you will hear a disgruntled intern say," I got scutted to death."

By the time you are an intern, you will hate to do these procedures, but you need to be capable of performing them. Some hospitals assign the nurses and other ancillary staff some of these tasks, and that may limit your access to these procedures. Do not let the fact that you are not responsible for scut keep you from learning these skills. Think this way: see one procedure, do one, and then teach one. If the nurses or ancillary staff do these procedures, ask them politely to teach you, and be thankful afterward.

And on the first day of the rotation, tell your intern you are interested in learning all these procedures. A student who can perform these skills will be appreciated by the team, and appreciation will lead to better evaluations. Having these skills also will make your transition from student to doctor less embarrassing. During your internship, the hospital will be expecting you to be able to complete these tasks. Do not let your rotation pass without being able to comfortably complete scut.

Should I carry any books with me?

Carry books that will fit easily in your lab coat. Don't carry books in your hand; you will lose them within a week. Some pocket-sized books I recommend are *Harrison's Pocket Principles of Internal Medicine* by Jean D. Wilson, M.D. et. al., *The Washington Manual by Michele*, M.D. et.al., and any book with dosages of the most commonly prescribed drugs. You will constantly have questions about patients, and you will not have time to complete a search in the library. These books will allow you to look up topics immediately. Your education and patients will benefit.

What do I put in an admit order?

The admit order is required for each patient being admitted to the hospital, and you will be writing them with your intern countersigning. Remember the admit order mnemonic ADC - VANDALISM

A - ADMIT - to which doctor's service: admit to Dr. Kim
D - Diagnosis
C - Condition on admission - stable, fair, critical
V - Vitals - how often you want vitals checked
A - Allergies
N - Nursing Notes - any special instructions for the nurses
D - Diet - NPO (nothing by mouth), Regular, Diabetic, Heart Smart
A - Activity - bed rest, full, as tolerated, etc.
L - Labs - what labs you would like drawn and when
I - IV - what fluid you want run and at what rate
S - Special Orders - any orders that do not fall into the other categories. For example, X-rays, echocardiogram, notify doctor if ...,
M - Medications - that you order for patient

Who are Osler, Laennec, Sutton, etc., and why do I hear their names?

Internal medicine physicians use eponyms for diseases and diagnostic symptomatology. These physicians had incredible careers and are considered pioneers of medicine. I believe many doctors want to keep the history and heritage alive in medicine, so they occasionally bring up these doctors' names. Also, physicians have learned diseases by their eponymonic name. So I will briefly tell you about some of these great figures in medicine along with concepts they're known for. I will also include a nonphysician, Willy Sutton, because you will hear the term Sutton's Law used on the floors.

Sutton's Law - to perform the diagnostic test or treatment most likely to establish the diagnosis. You will hear physicians tell you to "go where the money is" in terms of deciding a diagnosis for a patient. Willy Sutton was a successful American bank robber who was eventually caught and put in prison. When asked why he robbed banks, he stated, "Because that's where the money is."

Osler Nodes - painful indurated areas on the pads of the fingers seen in subacute bacterial endocarditis.

Sir William Osler (1849-1919) - Osler graduated from McGill University Medical School, and at 26 he was appointed Professor of the Institute of Medicine. Eventually he was recruited to John Hopkins as Professor of Medicine in 1889. Here he introduced the concept of bedside teaching. He was famous for inspiring young physicians and medical students. He wrote a book in 1892 called Principles and Practice of Medicine that was used by physicians everywhere. Osler wrote many essays and gave incredible speeches on medicine that I recommend medical students read. Here are some famous Osler quotes:

"To study medicine without reading textbooks is like going to sea without charts, but to study medicine without dealing with patients is not to go to sea at all."

"Things cannot always go your way. Learn to accept in silence the minor aggravations, cultivate the gift of taciturnity and consume your own smoke with an extra draught of hard work, so that those about you may not be annoyed with the dust and soot of your complaints."

Laennec Cirrhosis - micronodular cirrhosis most commonly associated with heavy alcoholic intake.

R.T.H. Laennec (1781-1826) - French physician. In 1816 he invented and named the stethoscope (Greek for examining the chest). He used a wooden cylinder 30 cm. long, putting one end by his ear and the other end to the chest. He introduced the terms pectoriloquy, rales, and egophony.

You will hear many more names and eponyms during your rotation. You will not have time to gather information about these famous physicians, but if you have the time, look up some of the writings of Osler, whose advice to students is as beneficial today as it was years ago.

The Surgery Clerkship

In surgery you will be called upon to complete pre-rounds, rounds, write notes, and present: in a similar way to your medicine rotation but you will also be involved in the operating room (O.R.). Some surgeries may last the whole day, so speed and efficiency in your non-O.R. duties is essential. You will notice that surgeons seem to do everything faster: rounds, notes, presentations, and even lunch. So they have enough time to complete rounds and still get to the operating room on time, they will round very early in the morning. Do not be surprised if you are asked to come into the hospital before 5 a.m. to pre-round. Be prepared for the increase in tempo because surgeons will not wait for you. You will either keep up or be left behind with a terrible evaluation.

How do I pre-round in surgery?

Pre-round on all your patients, but ask carefully focused questions. If your patient has an acute abdomen, performing a complete eye exam each morning would be worthless. Invoke Sutton's Law: Go to where the money is, and don't waste time with useless examinations.

On admission do a complete history and physical, but once you have determined that the other systems are in check, concentrate on the problem that concerns the surgeon. If a patient has other significant diseases that do not require a surgeon, let the internist on consult (consultants are physicians called by the primary caregiver to give their insight on a particular problem that falls in their field of specialty) worry about the nonsurgical pathology. Not unlike internal medicine this is a specialty in medicine. Your pre-round should include gathering all data including vital signs, labs, and radiological studies.

Pre-rounding on postsurgical patients requires extra questioning and work. For example, you will have specific questions for a patient who has undergone surgery of the abdomen. They may include: Have you passed gas? Do you feel any abdominal pain? Have you had any fever or chills during the night? Have you had a bowel movement? Have you urinated throughout the night? As a student, you will check for bowel sounds. You'll check the wound and change the dressing. You will also check the lungs of any postsurgical patient because these patients have a higher incidence of atelectasis due to the anesthesia.

You'll also check all intravenous lines for infiltration or signs of infection. You want accurate information about the patient's intake (IV or oral) and output (urine outflow). You must also pay close attention to vital signs to measure hemodynamic stability and monitor for post-surgical infection.

The surgical progress note

The surgical progress note is slightly different than the internal medicine progress note but you will still use the SOAP format. You will add information, but the notes will be shorter than your internal medicine notes.

S - Ask about pain, flatus, bowel movements, etc.

O- POD#- post operative day

S/P - status post operation

CVL - central venous line - how many days

Vitals including Tmax and Tmin, I/Os intake over output, drain output.

PE - include only those systems pertinent to disease and wound site

Lab and radiological findings

A/P- normal assessment and plan

How are rounds conducted?

Most of the time, rounds in surgery are conducted at the bedside. In medicine, you have three to five minutes to present the case. In surgery at best you'll be given one minute for a postsurgical case and maybe two minutes for a new case.

Example of a postsurgical presentation:

This is Mrs. Sanchez. She is a 24-year-old status post appendectomy yesterday. Pt. has been feeling minimal abdominal pain. She had a Tmax of 99.4 and a Tmin of 98. Her intake over output in the last 12 hours is 1200ccs over 900ccs. She had a bowel movement last night. On physical exam, patient had positive bowel sounds in all quadrants and minimal abdominal tenderness in the lower right quadrant. Wound is clean with no signs of infection. Pt. is status post appendectomy for appendicitis with no postsurgical complications. The plan is to continue present management and slowly advance oral intake.

If you are presenting a new patient, use the same format for presentation we discussed in the last chapter. Remember to focus more on the condition that requires a surgeon's care and only describe past medical history pertinent to the surgical pathology.

What will I be doing in the operating room?

You will be watching operations, pulling retractors, cutting knots, and trying not to break the sterile fields. You will be standing for hours in the O.R.. You will probably wonder what educational value it serves to stand and hold a retractor. To make the O.R. experience educational, ascertain the O.R. schedule for the next day. Look up the pathology, anatomy, and surgical principles involved in the operation. Anticipate the questions that the attending may ask you during the operation. During the operation ask yourself questions. Think of this internal questioning as mental gymnastics. If you don't do mental gymnastics, all you will learn in the O.R. is how to stand for hours without falling asleep.

You will be asked at times to suture and tie knots. Practice both techniques before you are called on to suture a person. Most surgery programs have knot-tying boards with instruction manuals.

Will I be writing any special orders or notes?

You will be writing admit orders. Use the ADC - VANDALISM format for the admission. In surgery you will write pre- and post-operation notes. Post-op notes can be remembered with the mnemonic PPP SAFE DCCS. (Say to yourself, "PPP safe docs.")

P - Pre-operative diagnosis
P - Procedure performed
P - Post-operative diagnosis
S - Surgeons
A - Anesthesia
F - Fluids - IV
E - Estimated blood loss
D - Drains - where have drains been placed
C - Complications

C - Condition

S - Specimens - any specimens sent to pathology

Pre-op notes are much simpler. They include all the results of tests that should be ordered before each surgery. Here's your mnemonic: PP-SACC-LEO

P - Pre-op diagnosis

P - Procedure

S - Surgeons

A - Allergies

C - Consent: patient's consent for the operation

C - CXR

L - Labs: chemistry, PT, PTT, CBC, platelets, UA

E - ECG

O - Orders: cleared medical conditions, blood type and cross units held

What should I carry with me?

Continue to carry your book of most commonly prescribed drugs. I also recommend the pocket-sized *Principles of Surgery* by Shwartz. Also, carry gauze, tape, an IV needle, and duoderm for dressing changes and IV placement.

The Obstetrics and Gynecology Clerkship

Obstetrics and gynecology will require you to adjust to a new way of conducting rounds and writing notes. The Ob/Gyn physicians use many abbreviations and acronyms. Your notes and admissions will be conducted and written differently. If your surgery and internal medicine clerkships precede Ob/Gyn, you will adjust well because you will have experience dealing with pathology and operating room techniques which will come in handy during labor and deliveries. Also, Ob/Gyn mirrors surgery with its gynecological operations and deliveries.

What abbreviations should I learn?

When you are writing notes or discussing patients you will be expected to write and talk in abbreviations and acronyms to save time. Here is a list of the most common ones:

A&O - alert and oriented

A&W - alive and well

BOWI - bag of water intact

CA - cancer C

C/S - cesarean section

C&S - culture and sensitivity

D&C - dilation and curettage
EBL - estimated blood loss
EDC - estimated date of confinement
EFW - estimated fetal weight
FH - fundal height
FT - full-term
FHT - fetal heart tones
LMP - last menstrual period
NSVD - normal spontaneous vaginal delivery
PID - pelvic inflammatory disease
POD - post-op day
PPD - postpartum day
PROM - premature rupture of membranes
PTL - preterm labor
RBOW - ruptured bag of water
Rh - rhesus factor positive or negative
SIUP - single intrauterine pregnancy
SOOL - spontaneous onset of labor
U/S - ultrasound
WDWN - well developed, well nourished
G and P:
   G - gravida = number of pregnancies including present
   P - para has four parts in order   F - full-term births
                                            P - preterm births
                                            A - abortions
                                                  (spontaneous and elective)
                                            L - living children

What changes do I make in my H and P?

You will still follow the CHAMP FASTS format. In the HPI, you must include the G and P, LMP, EDC, prenatal care, etc. Include prenatal vitamins in medications list for Ob patients and contraception in your Gyn patients. Your PMH will include Ob and Gyn history as well as the normal PMH. In the PE you will include an extensive write-up for the pelvic exam.

Are my progress notes and op notes different?

Ob/Gyns concentrate their exams and their write-ups to the gynecological surgery or delivery. You will still use the SOAP format. In the objective section, you will include PPD or POD, blood type, Rubella immune, Rhogam used or not, RPR, drains, etc.

Pre- and post-op notes, and admit orders will essentially be the same as those you completed for surgery.

The Psychiatry Clerkship

In psychiatry you will concentrate more on the psychosocial factors and social history. Instead of spending most of your time looking at lab results, standing in an operating room, or delivering babies in the middle of the night, in psychiatry your goal is to talk with the patient. The physical exam will be cursory at best; determining patients' mental status now becomes the focus. Your objective is to gather a thorough history. You will not be rushed for time.

You would have to deliberately try to receive a poor evaluation on your psychiatry rotation because the workload is less demanding than the other rotations. Even so, there are some things you can do to make the rotation more successful.

First, buy the *Pocket Handbook of Clinical Psychiatry* by Harold I. Kaplan, M.D. and Benjamin J. Sadock, M.D. Before the rotation begins, read the psychiatric examination chapter. Most programs have their own method of H and P write-ups, but you will ask all the questions in the Kaplan and Sadock book.

Second, ask if the department has a book on commonly prescribed psychiatric drugs produced and distributed free by a pharmaceutical company.

Finally, work to be at ease with patients, which will put your patients at ease and lead to better histories.

The Pediatrics Clerkship

In pediatrics you will be called upon to conduct physicals on uncooperative patients. Young children hate to be poked and prodded. So practice your patience and sense of humor. Take your time, and develop the confidence of both the parents and the child. You will be counting on the parents to provide the history and the child to stay still long enough for you to conduct an adequate physical. Children present a different set of common problems than do adults, and you will learn these as you complete the rotation.

For the history, again use the CHAMP FASTS format, with some additions.

Allergies - Ask about pets in the house. Sometimes allergies to household pets can be the cause of a child's illness.

Medications - immunization history

Past Medical History - Include the mnemonic BADDS for infants (birth to 1 year)

B - birth history
A - APGAR score
D - developmental stages
    lifting head
    sitting up
    talking
    walking
    running
D - diet
S - school history

Social History - Include the mnemonic HEADS for teenagers
H - home life
E - education (school life)
A - activities
D - drugs
S - sex and suicide

You'll conduct the physical differently with infants and young children than you did with adults. Leave the head as the last part of the physical because it is the most annoying part of the exam for children. Start with the lungs and heart. Then end your exam with the ears. If possible, let parents keep infants in their arms during the exam. Infants will be more relaxed and more cooperative.

During the rotation carry with you *The Harriet Lane Handbook*, which is a pediatric pocketbook that includes developmental charts, medications, growth charts, etc. Also carry a pocket calculator. You will be expected to carry out many calculations to determine weight-dependent calorie counts and drug dosages.

These are the core clerkships. Internal medicine, surgery, and obstetrics and gynecology received the most attention because these specialties require the most adjustment for students.

At the end of your third year you should have the confidence of a veteran. That means you will know your role in the hospital. You should have learned how to best deal with patients, peers, doctors, and all the other health care professionals. You should begin to feel that if a patient walked into the hospital you would be able to take care of them. In your fourth year you will be given more autonomy and responsibility. You will begin to make treatment decisions with the supervision of the doctors on your team. The end of the third year is an exciting time because you begin to see the light at the end of the tunnel.

Chapter 6

The Fourth Year

In your fourth year, you begin the transition from student to doctor. You will have increased responsibilities in the hospital. The team will expect you to handle more of the day-to-day work. Now you have the freedom to do elective clerkships instead of core clerkships. Elective clerkships are considered the fields in medicine that are specialties like dermatology, orthopedics, ophthalmology, radiology, cardiology, etc. You will still be required to do some core clerkships more in depth but most of your year will be spent in the specialties of your choice.

Some schools have fourth year core clerkships called sub-internships. You will be treated in these sub-internships like a doctor. In the sub-internships, the team expects you to keep pace independently without an intern. Let the added responsibility serve as preparation for your upcoming internship, where you will take on even more responsibility.

Choosing a Specialty

Not only will you have more responsibilities during your fourth year, but you will also choose a specialty and apply and interview for residencies. If you've followed my advice from the beginning of the book, you've already shadowed physicians in different specialties and requested information from their respective associations (Appendix 2). The specialties that interested you are the specialties in which you should rotate as electives. Use the elective as a final barometer for deciding whether you see yourself in that specialty.

Many books have advice on how to choose a specialty. Some books state that there are only a few specialties worth pursuing for financial reasons or quality of life issues (time spent working). Other books use a logical (even mathematical) approach to choosing a specialty. Still others advocate dividing the specialties into two groups: surgical and nonsurgical. These advocates maintain that once you choose one of these groups, the choice is like choosing between shades of gray.

I don't agree that there are only a few specialties worth pursuing. I find the mathematical approach good in some respects but not used by most doctors satisfied with their specialty choice. The surgical versus nonsurgical approach may be a good start, but the specific specialties within the two groups are vastly different, so you are still left with a difficult decision.

Most doctors I talked with stated three criteria in choosing their specialties: genuine interest in the information covered in their specialty, time spent working and how it fit their projected lifestyle, and enjoyment of the time they spent rotating through the specialty. I agree with the first two criteria for choosing a specialty, but I caution you on the third.

You should not choose a specialty based only on your rotation experience. You may enjoy your rotation experience for factors that have little to do with the specialty, like being placed on a good team, a smooth-running hospital, or a unique system of operation that fits your personality. All these factors may have made you enjoy a clerkship but it does not mean that you will like doing that particular specialty your entire life.

On the other hand, having bad experiences with a team causes many students to eliminate specialties they may have otherwise enjoyed.

For these reasons, I recommend looking instead at what physicians in particular specialties do on a day-to-day basis, and determine if you would enjoy completing these tasks. Again, shadowing physicians during the beginning of your medical school training will give you a more objective perspective than you'll get from rotations.

Whatever criteria you use to decide on a specialty, you will not have much time to decide if you wait until your fourth year. I have stated often the importance of planning early. In your M3 year, you will not have time to decide on a specialty unless you are considering one of the core clerkships. So start considering possibilities earlier in medical school: shadow physicians and request more information from the specialties' respective associations (Appendix 2).

USMLE 2 and Your Residency

Sometime during your fourth year, you will be responsible for USMLE 2. If you have prepared your review sheet and reviewed questions from previous exams (usually the examination registration packet includes a sample test with answers) you should be ready.

USMLE 2 is not used for residency selection like USMLE 1, except in some dermatology residencies. Even though the score will not count, you should still study intensely. Consider USMLE 2 your final exam in a long road to becoming a doctor. You might as well end as strongly as you started.

The National Residency Matching Program (NRMP)

The NRMP is the central service similar to AMCAS that handles the application process of students and residencies. All students applying for U.S. residencies must use NRMP. The exceptions are the specialties not handled by NRMP. Those specialties are neurology, neurosurgery, ophthalmology, otolaryngology, plastic surgery, and urology. NRMP residency spots are divided into categorical, advanced, preliminary, and transitional. The match for all programs, including non-NRMP specialties, is handled by a computer rank and match system. You submit a rank list from your first choice of residency to the last. The programs, in turn, rank students who they have interviewed from first, most desirable, to last. The computer matches you with your highest ranked program which in turn ranks you high. To better understand this matching process, here are some reading examples of how it might work.

*You rank a program as your top choice (number one). That program has three open residency spots. The program ranks you among the top three candidates. So you will receive your top choice.

*You rank a program as your top choice (number one). That program has three open residency spots. The program ranks you sixth. The first three people on their list matched in other programs that were their first choices? Again you will receive your top choice.

*You rank a program as your top choice (number one). That program has three open residency spots. They rank you fourth on that program's list. The first three people on their list all matched in this program. You will not receive your top choice, so the computer goes to the second choice on your list. The process begins again with your second choice.

The computer actually begins from your last choice and works its way up your rank order list. Each time you gain entrance into a higher ranked program, you relinquish your spot in the lower ranked program. Bottom line: You will receive your highest choice possible. Either the program will rank you in the top spots available or candidates ahead of you on the list will match in other programs they ranked higher, creating an opportunity for you to match.

There is no magic to the system, so don't bother trying to outsmart the computer. Rank the programs in your order of preference. If you have a number one choice, rank that program number one and so on. A rumor started before my class's match day that students always get their third choice, so everyone should put their first choice third. As we soon found out the rumor was not true; most of the students in our class received their first or second choice. Do not believe any of these match myths or rumors.

What is the Difference Between the Different Residency Categories?

Categorical position - a residency spot that you will have from the beginning until the end of your residency unless you transfer. For example, a categorical spot in Internal Medicine means that you will start in the program as a postgraduate Year 1 (PGY 1), progress to a PGY 3, and then graduate.

Advanced position - a position that you begin after completion of a preliminary year of some other specialty or a transitional year. For example, you apply now for an ophthalmology spot that will begin a year after graduation, provided that you complete a preliminary or transitional year.

Transitional year - one-year residency spot in which you rotate through a variety of specialties. The transitional year is used by those graduates who accepted an advanced spot, who did not match, or who want one year's experience before deciding on a specialty.

Preliminary year - one year contract in a defined specialty, such as surgery or internal medicine The preliminary year is used by graduates hoping to attain a categorical spot in that particular specialty either by way of someone dropping out of a program or by reapplying through the match. Another reason for completing a preliminary year is for the same reasons as completing a transitional year.

The steps for securing a residency, even for competitive residencies, take place before the application process. If you follow the steps in this book and work hard during your four years, you will acquire a good residency.

The process of residency selection mirrors the process of medical school selection. Use the same strategies you followed to attain an admission to medical school to match in a residency. For details on the process in the specialty of your choice, consult students from your school who have matched in the same specialty.

No matter when in the process you have bought this book, I hope it has helped you attain your goal. Being a doctor can be frustrating but rewarding. I encourage anyone with the desire and commitment to becoming a physician that goal because it is a fun job. You will feel needed by society, you will connect with people in a very personal way, you will use knowledge that you have learned in school and common sense that you have learned with life experience. As in any profession there are frustrations, but those are forgotten when a patient thanks you for a job well done.

I would love to hear what you think about the book and about your application and medical school adventures. You can e-mail me at ROS-TAR80@aol.com. Hope to hear from you. Good luck!

Part 2

Directory of
Medical Schools

This section includes in order: school name, web site, phone number, requirements for admission, AMCAS involvement, tuition for state residents (R) and non-residents (NR), and number of residents and non-residents accepted in the 1995-96 M1 class. Some entries will have information concerning the school that you cannot find out from a brochure. Abbreviations have been used. In the requirements section, letters stand for subjects; alone the letters stand for one year or two semesters or three quarters of the subject. For example, B alone stands for one year of biology. B = biology, IC = inorganic chemistry or general chemistry, OC = organic chemistry, P = physics, C = calculus, E = English, BS = behavioral science, SS = social science. If the school accepts AMCAS applications the letter Y is used. N means the school does not accept AMCAS, but instead have their own separate application.

You will notice that most schools do not require completion of baccalaureate degree for admission. All these schools state that an applicant who will have a degree at the time of admission is preferred. More than 93 percent of students have their baccalaureate degree before beginning medical school. No school requires that a student major in a particular subject.

Use the information provided as a starting point when choosing medical schools. You should call any school you are considering and request that they send you their school brochure and application material.

ALABAMA

Univ. of Alabama
http://www.1h1.uab.edu/uasom
Phone: 205-934-2330
Requirements: MCAT, 90 semester hrs., B, IC, OC, P, C, E
AMCAS: Y
Tuition: R $7,797 NR $19,213
M1 Class: R142 NR 23
First two years are completed in Birmingham. The next two years are done in Tuscaloosa, Birmingham, or Huntsville.

Univ. of South Alabama
http://www.usouthal.edu/usa/deps-grd.html
205-460-7176
MCAT, 90 semester hrs., B, IC, OC, P, E, C
Y
R $6,445 NR $12,223
R 57 NR 7

ARIZONA

Univ. of Arizona
http://zax.radiology.arizona.edu/intro.pic.html
602-626-6214
MCAT, B or Z, IC, OC, P, E, 90 semester hrs.
Must be a resident of Arizona, or WICHE certified
or funded residents from Alaska, Montana, Wyoming
Y
R $6,826 NR not available
R 98 NR 2

ARKANSAS

Univ. of Arkansas
http://amanda.uams.edu:80/uams.html
501-686-5354
MCAT, 90 semester hrs., B, IC, OC, P, M, E
Y
R $7,527 NR $14,871
R 139 NR 4

CALIFORNIA

Univ. of California, Davis
http://www.ucdmc.ucdavis.edu/
916-752-2717
MCAT, 90 semester hrs., E, B, IC, OC, P, C
Y
R $7,837 NR $15,536
R 90 NR 3

Univ. of California, Irvine
http://meded.com.uci.edu:80/
714-856-5388
MCAT, 3 yrs. undergraduate, B, IC, OC, P, C
Y
R $8,281 NR $15,980
R 92 NR 0
School has a peer tutoring program.

Univ. of California, Los Angeles
http://www.mednet.ucla.edu/som/
310-825-6081
MCAT, 3 yrs. undergraduate, E, P, IC, OC, B, M
Y
R $7,864 NR $15,563
R 157 NR 12

Univ. of California, San Diego
http://feedback@infopath.ucsd.edu
619-534-3880
MCAT, 3 yrs. college, at least one in 4 yr. university
B, IC, OC, P, M (calculus, stats, computer science)
Y
R $8,239, NR $15,938
R 117 NR 5

Univ. of California, San Francisco
http://www.reg.uci.edu/SANET/ucsf.html
415-476-4044
MCAT, 3 yrs. college, 90 semester units
Qtr. hrs. B 12, IC 12, OC 8, P 12
Y
R $7,696 NR $15,395
R 115 NR 38

Loma Linda University
http://www.llu.edu
909-824-4467
MCAT, 90 semester hrs., B, IC, OC, P, E
Y
R and NR $22,788
R 84 NR 75

Univ. of Southern California
http://www.usc.edu/hsc/med-sch/
213-342-2552
MCAT, 4 yrs. or 120 semester hrs., B, IC, OC, P
Y
R and NR $26,520
R 126 NR 24

Stanford University
http://www-med.stanford.edu/
415-723-6861
MCAT, B, IC, OC, P
Y
R and NR $24,375
R 48 NR 38

COLORADO

Univ. of Colorado
http://www.uchsc.edu/sm/sm
303-270-7361
MCAT, degree or 120 semester units, B, IC, OC
P, M 6 semester hrs., E lit. 6 hrs., E comp. 3 hrs.
R $12,150 NR $19,562
R 106 NR 23

CONNECTICUT

Univ. of Connecticut
http://www.uchc.edu
203-679-2152
MCAT, 3 yrs. college, B, IC, OC, P
Y
R $11,350 NR $21,700
R 72 NR 11

Yale University
http://info.med.yale.edu/medadmit
203-785-2643
MCAT, B or Z, IC, OC, P
N
R and NR $23,300
R 13 NR 88
Many graduates stay in academic medicine. Yale students are responsible for themselves, to the point where they must identify themselves to the course director if they are failing. There are no grades at Yale.

DISTRICT OF COLUMBIA

George Washington University
http://www.gwu.edu/~gwumc/medschool.html
202-994-3506
MCAT, 3 yrs. college, 90 semester units
B, IC, OC, P, E 6 semester units
Y
R and NR $30,932
R 19 NR 139

Georgetown University
http://www.dml.georgetown.edu/schmed
202-687-1154
MCAT, 90 semester hrs., B, IC, OC, P, M, E
Y
R and NR $23,625
R 2 NR 163

Howard University
http://www.cldc.howard.edu/~bhlogan/hucm-cat.html
202-806-6270
MCAT, 62 semester hrs., B, IC, OC, P,
6 semester hrs. college M and E
R and NR $14,805
R 4 NR 107

FLORIDA

Univ. of Florida
http://www.med.ufl.edu/
904-392-4569
MCAT, degree, B, IC, OC, P
Y
R $8,173 NR $21,172
R 110 NR 5
Tuition has remained stable over the last three years.

Univ. of Miami
http://www.med.miami.edu
305-547-6791
MCAT, 90 semester hrs., 6 semester hrs. E, B or Z, other science courses
IC, OC, P
Y
R and NR $23,040
R 136 NR 2

Univ. of South Florida
http://com1.med.usf.edu/
813-974-2229
MCAT, 3 yrs. college, B, IC, OC, P, M, E
Y
R $8,261 NR $21,261
R 96 NR 1 NR are discouraged from applying

GEORGIA

Emory University
http://www.emory.edu/
404-727-5660
MCAT, 3 yrs. college, 90 semester hrs.
B, IC, OC, P, E 6 semester hrs.
18 semester hrs. of humanities, social and/or behavioral sciences
Y
R and NR $20,710
R 61 NR 53

Medical College of Georgia
http://www.mcg.edu/
706-721-4792
MCAT, B, IC, advanced chemistry, P, E,
Y
R $4,755 NR $14,976
R 176 NR 4

Mercer University
http://gain.mercer.peachnet.edu/www/famnet.html
912-752-2542
MCAT, 90 semester hrs., B, IC, OC, P
Y
R and NR $18,890
R 55 NR 0

Morehouse School of Medicine
http://www.msm.edu/
404-752-1650
MCAT, 90 semester hrs., B, IC, OC, P
6 semester hrs. M, E
Y
R and NR $15,750
R 26 NR 8

HAWAII

Univ. of Hawaii
http://medworld.biomed.hawaii.edu/ome.html
808-956-5446
MCAT, 90 semester hrs., B or Z, C 12-16 semester hrs.
physics
Y
R $6,083 NR $21,117
R 44 NR 12

ILLINOIS

Univ. of Chicago
http://ap-www.uchicago.edu/AcaPubs/GradAnno/bsd95/22bs-pritz.html
312-702-1939
MCAT, 90 semester hrs., B, IC, OC, P
Y
R and NR $22,178
R 42 NR 62
Most graduates pursue academic medicine. Financial aid is need blind, meaning need is not considered when allocating funds. The new facilities (3 years old) are comfortable.

Chicago Medical School
708-578-3206
MCAT, 3 yrs. college, 135 quarter hrs.
B or Z, IC, OC, P
Y
R and NR $29,106
R 49 NR 119
The school accepts a high percentage of California residents.

Univ. of Illinois
http://www.uic.edu/depts/mcam/
312-996-5635
MCAT, legal residents of U.S., college degree
Y
R $10,738 NR $28,958
R 304 NR 13
Largest medical school in the country with 300 students divided into two campuses (Chicago and Urbana-Champaign). Tuition waivers for research. Recently, they opened a new student lounge and computer center.

Loyola Univ. Chicago Stritch
http://www.meddean.luc.edu
708-216-3229
MCAT, bachelor's degree, B, IC, OC, P
Y
R $20,900 NR $25,600
R 65 NR 65

Northwestern University
http://www.nums.nwu.edu/
312-503-8206
MCAT, 90 semester hrs.
Y
R and NR $25,446
R 81 NR 93
Located in the heart of downtown Chicago. Northwestern offers debt capping which means the school will pay for a student's debt above a calculated amount depending on the classes available funds and collective need. The school recently opened a modern computer lab. Also, the school is building a $580 million hospital to open in 1999.

Rush Medical College
http://www.rpslmc.edu/
312-942-6913
MCAT, 90 semester hrs., B, IC, OC, P
Y
R and NR $22,944
R 104 NR 16

Southern Illinois University
http://www.c-som.siu.edu/
217-782-2860
MCAT, 90 semester hrs.
Y
R $11,295 NR $31,365
R 72 NR 1
The noncompetitive pass/fail system has most students agreeing that there is not a distracting competition among students. Curriculum geared towards producing primary care physicians. The school has obtained a new women's and children's hospital.

INDIANA

Indiana University
http://www.iupui.edu/it/medschl/home.html
317-274-3772
MCAT, 90 semester hrs., B, IC, OC, P
Y
R $10,189 NR $22,764
R 258 NR 22

IOWA

Univ. of Iowa
http://www.medadmin.uiowa.edu/
319-335-8052
MCAT, 94 semester hrs., 4 yrs. college
B or Z, IC, OC, P, M
Y
R $8,600 NR $22,420
R 149 NR 26

KANSAS

Univ. of Kansas
http://www.kumc.edu/som/som.html_
913-588-5245
MCAT, bachelor's degree, B, IC, OC, P, E
1 semester C, or stats, or computer science
Y
R $8,802 NR $20,986
R 161 NR 14
Reduction in tuition over the last year.

KENTUCKY

Univ. of Kentucky
http://www.uky.edu/CollegeOfMedicine/
606-323-6161
MCAT, B, IC, OC, P, E
Y
R $8,479 NR $18,699
R 84 NR 11
School is looking for students who will eventually practice in Kentucky.

Univ. of Louisville
http://www.louisville.edu/medschool/
502-852-5193
MCAT, 90 semester hrs., B, IC, OC, P
M or 1 semester of C, E
Y
R $8,300 NR $18,520
R 122 NR 14

LOUISIANA

Louisiana State University in New Orleans
http://www.lsumc.edu/campus/welcome.htm
504-568-6262
MCAT, B, IC, OC, P
Y
R $6,774 NR $14,676
R 174 NR 1

Louisiana State University in Shreveport
http://www.lsumc.edu/?
318-674-5190
MCAT, 90 semester hrs., B or Z, IC, OC, P
E in 6 semester hrs.
Y
R $6,776 NR $14,676
R 101 NR O

Tulane University
http://www.mcl.tulane.edu
504-588-5187
MCAT, 90 semester hrs., B, IC, OC, P
E 6 semester hrs.
Y
R and NR $25,791
R 33 NR 115

MARYLAND

Johns Hopkins University
http://infonet.welch.jhu.edu/education/prospectives.html
410-955-3182
SAT or ACT or GRE - MCAT
may be used as substitute
B, IC, OC, P, C 4 semester hrs.
humanities 24 semester hrs.
N
R and NR $21,800
R 18 NR 101

Univ. of Maryland
http://www.som1.ab.umd.edu/som.html
410-706-7478
MCAT, 90 semester hrs., B, IC, OC, P, E
Y
R $12,257 NR $22,357
R 121 NR 25

Uniformed Services Univ. of the Health Sciences
http://www.usuhs.mil
800-772-1743 301-295-3101
U.S. citizens 18 to 30
meet physical and personal qualifications of uniformed services
MCAT, bachelor's degree, B, IC, OC, P, C 3 semester hrs.
E 6 semester hrs.
Tuition - None, but military obligation
R 11 NR 153

MASSACHUSETTS

Boston University
http://med-amsa.bu.edu
617-638-4630
MCAT, bachelor's degree, B, IC, OC, P, E, H
Y
R and NR $30,675
R 44 NR 99

Harvard Medical School
http://www.med.harvard.edu/programs/
617-432-1550
MCAT, 3 yrs. college, B, IC, OC, P, C 1 yr., E
N
R and NR $24,729
R 18 NR 149
Encourages students to defer entrance for one year.

Univ. of Massachusetts
http://www.ummed.edu:8000/
508-856-2323
MCAT, bachelor's degree, B, IC, OC, P, E
Y
R $10,597 NR N/A
R 100 NR 0

Tufts University
http://www.nemc.org/tusm/Welcome.html
617-956-6571
MCAT, 3 yrs. college, B, IC, OC, P
Y
R and NR $30,810
R 52 NR 124

MICHIGAN

Michigan State University
http://www.chm.msu.edu/CHM_HTML/CHM_Home_Page.html
517-353-9620
MCAT, 3 yrs. college, B, IC, OC, P, E
psychology or sociology 6 semester hrs., nonscience 18 semester hrs.
Y
R $14,058 NR $29,904
R 79 NR 25

Univ. of Michigan
http://www.med.umich.edu/
313-764-6317
MCAT, 90 semester hrs., B 6 semester hrs.
IC, OC, biochemistry, P 6 semester hrs., E 6 semester hrs.
nonscience 18 hrs.
Y
R $16,216 NR $25,316
R 106 NR 59

Wayne State University
http://www.phymac.med.wayne.edu/offices.htm
313-577-1466
MCAT, 3 yrs. college, B or Z 12 semester hrs.
IC, OC, P, E
Y
R $9,916 NR $19,411
R 231 NR 16

MINNESOTA

Mayo Medical School
http://www.mayo.edu/education/rst/gsm.html
507-284-3671
MCAT, bachelor's degree, B, IC, OC, P, biochemistry
Y
R of Arizona, Florida, Minnesota $9,925
NR $19,800
R 10 NR 30
All students receive $10,270 grant and merit scholarship

Univ. of Minnesota,, Duluth
http://www.d.umn.edu/medweb/
218-726-8511
MCAT, bachelor's degree, B, IC, OC, P, E 6 semester hrs.
H, BS, M (calculus or stats)
Y
R $15,052 NR $29,548
R 46 NR 6

Univ. of Minnesota, Minneapolis
http://www.med.umn.edu/
612-624-1122
MCAT, bachelor's degree, in quarters B or Z,
IC, OC, P 3 quarters, BS, social science or other liberal arts
27 quarters, calculus or stats
Y
R $15,201 NR $26,697
R 170 NR 15

MISSISSIPPI

Univ. of Mississippi
http://fiona.umsmed.edu/
601-984-5010
MCAT, 3 yrs. college, B, IC, OC, P, advanced science
M and E 6 semester hrs.
Y
R $6,710 NR $12,710
R 100 NR 0

MISSOURI

Univ. of Missouri, Columbia
http://www.hsc.missouri.edu/som/docs/somadd.html
314-882-2923
MCAT, 90 semester hrs., B, IC, OC, P
college algebra or C, E comp. 6 semester hrs.
Y
R $12,647 NR $24,178
R 91 NR 1

Univ. of Missouri, Kansas City
http://research.med.umkc.edu
816-235-1870
Six-year program - bachelor's to M.D.
Call for more information.

Saint Louis University
http://www.slu.edu/colleges/med/
314-577-8205
MCAT, 3 yrs. college, B, IC, OC, P
E 6 semester hrs., other H or BS 12 semester hrs.
Y
R and NR $25,224
R 43 NR 109

Washington University
http://medschool.wustl.edu/admissions/
314-362-6857
MCAT, 3 yrs. college, B, IC, OC, P, M
Y
R and NR $25,170
R 12 NR 110

NEBRASKA

Creighton University
http://medicine.creighton.edu/
402-280-2798
MCAT, 3 yrs. college, B, IC, OC, P, E 6 semester hrs.
Y
R and NR $23,070
R 18 NR 94

Univ. of Nebraska
http://www.unmc.edu/
402-559-4205
MCAT, 90 semester hrs., B, IC, OC, P
H 12 semester hrs., C or stats
E comp
Y
R $10,550 NR $20,300
R 116 NR 3
Failure rate for national Boards part 1 was 18 percent in 1994 and 11 percent in 1995. National Average for Boards part 1 is 6-8 percent. School is increasing its review hours to help raise scores.

NEVADA

Univ. of Nevada
http://www.med.unr.edu/homepage/ome/
702-784-6063
MCAT, 90 semester hrs., B 12 semester hrs.
IC, OC, P, BS 6 semester hrs.
Y
R $8,715 NR $17,976
R 38 NR 14

NEW HAMPSHIRE

Dartmouth Medical School
http://griffith.dartmouth.edu
603-650-1505
MCAT, C, B, IC, OC, P
Y
R and NR $26,710
R 12 NR 79

NEW JERSEY

Univ. of Medicine and Dentistry of New Jersey
http://www2.umdnj.edu/rwjms.html
201-982-4631
MCAT, 3 yrs. college (90 semester hrs.)
B, IC, OC, P, E 6 semester hrs.
Y
R $13,680 NR $17,676
R 154 NR 16

Univ. of Medicine and Dentistry of New Jersey
Robert Wood Johnson Medical School
908-235-4576
MCAT, 3 yrs. college (90 semester hrs.)
B, IC, OC, P, M 1 semester, E
Y
R $14,512 NR $18,632
R 126 NR 12

NEW MEXICO

Univ. of New Mexico
505-277-4766
MCAT, 3 yrs. college, B, IC, OC, P
Y
R $4,899 NR $13,986
R 66 NR 7

NEW YORK

Albany Medical College
http://www.albanyanesth.com/index.htm
518-262-5521
MCAT, 3 yrs. college, B, IC, OC, P
Y
R $24,074 NR $25,346
R 52 NR 83
Students love the fact that the school is located close to New York City, Boston, and Montreal.

Albert Einstein College of Medicine
http://www.aecom.yu.edu/
718-430-2106
MCAT, 3 yrs. college, B, IC, OC, P
6 semester hrs. M and E
Y
R and NR $22,400
R 87 NR 89

Columbia University

http://cpmcnet.columbia.edu/dept/ps/
212-305-3595
MCAT, 3 yrs. college, B, IC, OC, P, E
Y
R and NR $25,750
R 37 NR 113

Cornell University Medical College

http://www.med.cornell.edu/
212-746-1067
MCAT, 3 yrs. college, B, IC, OC, P, E
all courses 6 semester hrs.
Y
R and NR $22,925
R 40 NR 61

Mount Sinai School of Medicine

http://www.mssm.edu
212-241-6696
MCAT, 3 yrs. college, B, IC, OC, P, M, E
Y
R and NR $21,825
R 71 NR 45
See New York University.

New York Medical College

914-993-4507
MCAT, bachelor's degree, B, IC, OC, P, E 6 semester hrs.
Y
R and NR $26,730
R 43 NR 145

New York University

http://www.med.nyu.edu/HomePage.html
212-263-5290
MCAT, 3 yrs. college, B, IC, OC, P, E
all courses 6 semester hrs.
N
R and NR $23,970
R 68 NR 91
Recently merged with Mount Sinai medical school. Strong general surgery and internal medicine departments. Students are very happy with a brand new living complex.

Univ. of Rochester

http://www.urmc.rochester.edu/urmc/welcome.htm
716-275-4539
MCAT not required, but if taken scores should be submitted
3 yrs. college, B, IC, OC, P, E all 6-8 semester hrs.
H or SS or BS 12-16 semester hrs.
N
R and NR $24,380
R 35 NR 63

State University of New York

Health Science Center at Brooklyn
http://www.hscbklyn.edu/
718-270-2446
MCAT, 3 yrs. college, B, IC, OC, P, E
Y
R $11,060 NR $22,160
R 181 NR 5

State University of New York at Buffalo

http://wings.buffalo.edu/smbs/
716-829-3465
MCAT, 3 yrs. college, B, IC, OC 1 semester, P, E
Y
R $11,641 NR $22,741
R 137 NR 2

State University of New York

Health Science Center at Syracuse
http://www.hscsyr.edu
315-464-4570
MCAT, 90 semester hrs., B, IC, OC, P 6-8 semester hrs.
E 6 semester hrs.
Y
R $11,055 NR $22,055
R 139 NR 7

Univ. at Stony Brook

School of Medicine / Health Science Center
http://www.grad.sunysb.edu/
516-444-2113
Y
R $10,990 NR $22,090
R 92 NR 8

NORTH CAROLINA

Bowman Gray School of Medicine
of Wake Forest University
http://isnet.is.wfu.edu/
910-716-4264
MCAT, 90 semester hrs., B, IC, OC, P
Y
R and NR $18,500
R 61 NR 47

Duke University
http://www.mc.duke.edu/depts/som/
919-684-2985
MCAT, 90 semester hrs., 3 yrs. college
B, IC, OC, P, C, E
Y
R and NR $22,400
R 33 NR 67

East Carolina University
http://www.med.ecu.edu/
919-816-2202
MCAT, 3 yrs. college, B or Z, IC, OC, P, E
Y
R $2,785 NR $21,299
R 72 NR 0

Univ. of North Carolina at Chapel Hill
http://www.med.unc.edu/
919-962-8331
MCAT, 96 semester hrs., B or Z, IC, OC, P
E 6 semester hrs.
Y
R $2,685 NR $21,200
R 143 NR 17

NORTH DAKOTA

Univ. of North Dakota
http://www.med.und.nodak.edu/
701-777-4221
MCAT, 90 semester hrs., B, IC, OC, P
college algebra 3 semester hrs., psychology or sociology 3 semester hrs.
E 6 semester hrs., semester of biochemistry may sub for semester OC
N
R $9,153 NR $23,281
R 43 NR 16

OHIO

Case Western Reserve University
http://www.cwru.edu/CWRU/med.html
216-368-3450
MCAT, 3 yrs. college, B, IC, OC, P
a class with significant writing content
Y
R and NR $23,890
R 82 NR 56
Curriculum and faculty geared towards graduating primary care
physicians.

Univ. of Cincinnati
http://www.med.uc.edu/htdocs/medicine/uccom.htm
513-558-7314
MCAT, 90 semester hrs., B, IC, OC, P, M
Y
R $11,037 NR $19,365
R 133 NR 27
Most students go into primary care.

Medical College of Ohio
http://www.mco.edu/
419-381-4229
MCAT, college degree, B, IC, OC, P, M, E
Y
R $10,223 NR $13,652
R 120 NR 20

Northeastern Ohio Universities
http://www.neoucom.edu
216-325-2511
MCAT, 3 yrs. college, OC, P
The program mainly B.S.-M.D.
Y
R $10,416 NR $20,133
R 94 NR 6

Ohio State University
http://bones.med.ohio-state.edu/homepage.html
614-292-7137
MCAT, bachelor's degree, B, IC, OC, P
Y
R $9,408 NR $26,694
R 167 NR 43

Wright State University
http://www.med.wright.edu
513-873-2934
MCAT, 3 yrs. college, 90 semester hrs.
B, IC, OC, P, M, E
Y
R $11,205 NR $15,075
R 78 NR 12

OKLAHOMA

Univ. of Oklahoma
http://www.online.uokhsc.edu/colleges/medicine/
405-271-2331
MCAT, 90 semester hrs., B or Z, IC, OC, P
3 semesters in E, and H or psychology, or sociology
anthropology, or foreign language
Y
R $7,875 NR $18,983
R 132 NR 17
All students finish their first year in Oklahoma with some moving to Tulsa for their clinical years. Strong departments include Internal medicine and Ob/Gyn. Many state-supported scholarships available.

OREGON

Oregon Health Sciences University
http://www.ohsu.edu/
503-494-2998
MCAT, bachelor's degree, B, IC, OC, P
one course M, 1 yr. H, SS, E
Y
R $14,970 NR $29,862
R 72 NR 24

PENNSYLVANIA

Jefferson Medical College
of Thomas Jefferson Univ.
http://jeffline.tju.edu/CWIS/JMC/jmc.html
215-955-6983
MCAT, 3 yrs. college, 90 semester hrs.
B, IC, OC, P
Y
R and NR $24,500
R 90 NR 133
Located in the business district of Philadelphia. Students have clinical experience in the first two years. Strong programs include orthopedics, ophthalmology, ENT, and rehabilitation. Students are graded with a traditional numerical grading system.

Medical College of Pennsylvania
and Hahnemann Univ. School of Medicine / merged to become Allegheny Health Education and Research Foundation
http://www.allegheny.edu/homepage.html
215-991-8202
MCAT, 90 semester hrs., B, IC, OC, P, E
Y
R and NR $23,00
R 134 NR 106

Pennsylvania State University
http://www.hmc.psu.edu/
717-531-8755
MCAT, 3 yrs. college, B, IC, OC, P
Y
R $15,724 NR $22,642
R 59 NR 60

Univ. of Pennsylvania
http://www.med.upenn.edu
215-898-8001
MCAT, bachelor's degree
Call admissions office for more information.
Y
R and NR $25,713
R 41 NR 110
Offers dual degrees like MD/MBA and DDS/MD. Well-known for its research facilities.

Univ. of Pittsburgh
http://www.omed.pitt.edu/~omed/homepage2.html
412-648-9891
MCAT, 120 semester hrs., B, IC, OC, P, E
Y
R $18,170 NR $24,299
R 86 NR 55

Temple University
http://www.temple.edu/medschool/TUSM.html
215-707-3656
MCAT, 3 yrs. college, B, IC, OC, P
H 6 semester hrs.
Y
R $20,550 NR $25,653
R 107 NR 80

PUERTO RICO

Universidad Central del Caribe
809-740-1611 ext. 210
MCAT, 90 semester hrs., B or Z, IC, OC, P
M, E, Spanish 6 semester hrs.
BS or SS, or H 6 semester hrs.
R $15,000 NR $22,000
R 53 NR 7

Ponce School of Medicine
http://wwwrcm.upr.clu.edu/
809-840-2511
MCAT, 90 semester hrs., B, IC, OC, P
M 6 semester hrs., H 6 semester hrs.
E and S 12 semester hrs.
Y
R $17,480 NR $25,311
R 43 NR 17

Univ. of Puerto Rico
809-758-2525
MCAT, 90 semester hrs., B, IC, OC, P
Fluency in English and Spanish
E and S 12 semester hrs.
BS and SS 6 semester hrs.
Y
R $5,800 NR $10,800
R 111 NR 4

RHODE ISLAND

Brown University
http://biomedcs.biomed.brown.edu/Medschool/intro.html
401-863-2149
MCAT, Used as guidelines B, P, SS, BS
1 semester each biochemistry, C, stats and probability
IC, OC
N
R and NR $24,893
Majority of class in eight-year program.

SOUTH CAROLINA

Medical Univ. of South Carolina
http://www2.musc.edu
803-792-3281
MCAT, 90 semester hrs., no specific course
requirements
Y
R $6,304 NR $17,260
R 127 NR 13

Univ. of South Carolina
http://www.med.sc.edu/
803-733-3325
MCAT, 90 semester hrs., B, IC, OC, P
M and E 6 semester hrs.
Y
R $7,290 NR $18,620
R 64 NR 8

SOUTH DAKOTA

Univ. of South Dakota
http://www.usd.edu/med/index.html
605-677-5233
MCAT, 3 yrs. college, 90 semester hrs.
B or Z, IC, OC, P, M
Y
R $10,614 NR $21,417
R 42 NR 9

TENNESSEE

East Tennessee State University
James H. Quillen College of Medicine
615-929-6221
MCAT, 90 semester hrs., B, IC, OC, P
communications skills courses 9 semester hrs.
Y
R $8,908 NR $15,884
R 51 NR 9

Meharry Medical College
http://ccmac.mmc.edu
615-327-6223
MCAT, 3 yrs. college, B or Z, IC, OC, P
E 6 semester hrs.
Y
R and NR $19,664
R 9 NR 71

Univ. of Tennessee, Memphis
http://utmgopher.utmem.edu/imagemap/1med.html
901-448-5559
MCAT, 90 semester hrs., B, IC, OC, P
E 6 semester hrs., electives 52
R $8,836 NR $16,266
R 151 NR 14

Vanderbilt University
http://www.mc.vanderbilt.edu/vumc/index.html
615-322-2145
MCAT, bachelor's degree, B, IC, OC, P
E 6 semester hrs.
Y
R and NR $21,202
R 10 NR 93

TEXAS

Baylor College of Medicine
http://www.bcm.tmc.edu/
713-798-4841
MCAT, 90 semester hrs., B, IC, OC, P, E
N
R $8,879 NR $21,979
R 123 NR 45

Texas A&M University Health Science Center
http://thunder.tamu.edu
409-845-7744
MCAT, 60 semester hrs., B + 1/2 yr., IC, OC, P, E
1/2 yr. C
N
R $8,004 NR $21,104
R 64 NR 0

Texas Tech University
Health Science Center
http://www.ttuhsc.edu/
806-743-2997
MCAT, 90 semester hrs., B or Z 2 yrs.
IC, OC, P, E
N
R $7,650 NR $20,750
R 116 NR 4

Univ. of Texas
Southwestern Medical Center at Dallas
http://www.swmed.edu/
214-648-2670
MCAT, 90 semester hrs., B 2 yrs.
IC, OC, P, C 1/2 yr., E
N
R $7,084 NR $20,184
R 174 NR 25

Univ. of Texas
Medical School at Galveston
http://www.utmb.edu/
409-772-3517
MCAT, 90 semester hrs., B 2 yrs.
IC, OC, P, C 1/2 yr., E
N
R $6,993 NR $20,093
R 188 NR 12

Univ. of Texas
Houston Medical School
http://www.med.uth.tmc.edu/
713-792-4711
MCAT, 90 semester hrs., B 14 semester hrs.
IC, OC, P, C 3 semester hrs., E 6 semester hrs.
N
R $7,202 NR $20,302
R 183 NR 17

Univ. of Texas
Medical School at San Antonio
http://www.uthscsa.edu/
210-567-2665
MCAT, 90 semester hrs., B 14 semester hrs.
IC, OC, P, C 3 semester hrs., E 6 semester hrs.
N
R $7,065 NR $20,165
R 181 NR 20

UTAH

Univ. of Utah
School of Medicine
http://www.med.utah.edu/
801-581-7498
MCAT, IC, OC, P, E
Y
R $6,927 NR $14,760
R 75 NR 25

VERMONT

Univ. of Vermont
http://salus.uvm.edu/
802-656-2154
MCAT, 3 yrs. college, B or Z
IC, OC, P
Y
R $14,685 NR $27,185
R 31 NR 62

VIRGINIA

Eastern Virginia Medical School
of the Medical College of Hampton Roads
http://www.evms.edu/
804-446-5812
MCAT, 100 semester hrs., B, IC, OC, P
Y
R $13,000 NR $23,000
R 76 NR 25

Virginia Commonwealth University
Medical College of Virginia
http://views.vcu.edu/html/mcvhome.cgi
804-786-9629
MCAT, 90 semester hrs., B, IC, OC, P, E, M
Y
R $10,445 NR $24,676
R 124 NR 50

Univ. of Virginia
http://views.vcu.edu/html/schofmed.html
804-924-5571
MCAT, 90 semester hrs., B, IC, OC, P
Y
R $9,406 NR $21,380
R 98 NR 41

WASHINGTON

Univ. of Washington
http://www.hslib.washington.edu/hsc/som.html
206-543-7212
MCAT, under exceptional circumstances GRE
B, C 12 semester hrs., P 4 semester hrs., other science 8 semester hrs.
Y
R $7,752 NR $19,686
R 157 NR 9

WEST VIRGINIA

Marshall University
http://medicus.marshall.edu/
304-696-7312
MCAT, 3 yrs. college, B or Z, IC, OC, P
E and BS or SS 6 semester hrs.
Y
R $8,103 NR $18,315
R 45 NR 4

West Virginia University
http://www.hsc.wvu.edu/som/
304-293-3521
MCAT, 90 semester hrs., B, IC, OC, P
E and BS or SS 6 semester hrs.
Y
R $7,980 NR $19,714
R 83 NR 3

WISCONSIN

Medical College of Wisconsin
http://www.mcw.edu/
414-257-8246
MCAT, 90 semester hrs., B, IC, OC, P
E 6 semester units, high school or college algebra
Y
R $12,894 NR $22,985
R 92 NR 112

Univ. of Wisconsin Medical School
http://www.biostat.wisc.edu/homepage.html
608-263-4925
MCAT, 90 semester hrs., B or Z, IC, OC, P, M
Y
R $13,041 NR $18,895
R 115 NR 28

Appendix 2

For More Information

These sources should be able to provide answers to any questions you may have concerning entrance into residency programs and certification. You will receive information on newsletters, annual meetings and insight into a particular specialty.

Attn. Dr. Kahn
America Academy of Family Physicians
8880 Ward Pkwy.
Kansas City, MO 64114
816-333-9700

For Internal Medicine:

Attn. Glynis Rhodes
American College of Physicians
6th St. at Race St.
Philadelphia, PA 19106
215-351-2559

or

Attn. Tracy Cullen
American Society of Internal Medicine
2011 Pennsylvannia Ave. NW Suite 800
Washington, DC 20006
202-835-2746 Ext. 297

Attn. Lisa Stevens
American College of Surgeons
Communications Department
55 East Erie St.
Chicago, IL 60611
312-664-4050

Resource Center
American College of Obstetrics and
    Gynecologists
409 12th St. SW
Washington, DC 20024
202-638-5577

Attn. Mary Back
Academy of Pediatrics
141 Northwest Point Blvd.
Elk Grove Village, IL 60009
708-228-5005
800-433-9016

Public Affairs Office
American Psychiatric Assn.
1400 K St. NW
Washington, DC 20005
202-682-6220

American College of Radiology
Public Relations Dept.
1891 Preston White Dr.
Reston, VA 22091
703-648-8900

Attn. Ellen Winogrond
American Academy of Ophthalmology
655 Beach St./P.O. Box 7424
San Francisco, CA 94120-7424
415-561-8500

American Academy of Orthopaedic Surgeons
6300 North River Rd.
Rosemont, IL 60018-4262
708-823-7186

Attn: Donna Payne, Membership Dept.
American Academy of Otolaryngology
Head and Neck Surgery
1 Prince St.
Alexandria, VA 22314
703-836-4444

Attn: Jan Glas
College of American Pathologists
325 Waukegan Rd.
Northfield, IL 60093-2750
708-446-8800

American College of Cardiology
9111 Old Georgetown Rd.
Bethesda, MD 20014
301-897-5400

Attn: Marilyn Bade
American Society of Anesthesiologists
520 North West Hwy
Park Ridge, IL 60068
708-825-5586

American College of Emergency Physicians
Membership Dept.
P.O. Box 619911
Dallas, TX 75261
214-550-0911
800-798-1822

American Academy of Neurology
2221 University Ave. S.E.,
Suite 335
Minneapolis, MN 55414

American Urological Association
1120 North Charles St.
Baltimore, MD 21201
410-727-1100

Attn. Robin Mcquiston
American Academy of Allergy and Immunology
611 East Wells St.
Milwaukee, WI 53202
414-272-6071

Attn. Sharon Plenner
Plastic Surgery Educational Foundation
American Society of Plastic and Reconstructive Surgeons
444 East Algonquin Rd.
Arlington Heights, IL 60005
708-228-9900

Attn. Wendell Bostelmann
American Academy of Dermatology
P.O. Box 4014
Schaumburg, IL 60168-4014
708-330-0230

Attn. Dawn Levreau
American Academy of Physical Medicine and Rehabilitation
122 South Michigan Ave.,
Suite 1300
Chicago, IL 60603
312-922-9366

Part 3

Boards and Clerkship Review

These notes should be used as a review for clerkship tests and Boards parts two and three. As in any review book, the content is not a complete review of all the information you are responsible for after completion of your clerkships. I cover topics that appear frequently on tests and during rounds with attendings. Common abbreviations are used throughout the review for conciseness.

PEDIATRICS

Major developmental events
Birth - new born sleeps most of time
6 weeks - smiles when spoken to, lies flat on his abdomen
3 months - smiles spontaneously, follows objects with eyes
6 months - sits with support, rolls over
9 months - crawls, says mama and dada, holds his bottle
1 year - walks with hand held, speaks several words
18 months - walks well, can climb stairs, 10 words
2 years - runs, puts on simple clothing, two- or three-word sentences
3 years - rides tricycle
4 years - throws ball overhand, hops on one foot, toilet trained
5 years - copies triangle, dresses and undresses without assistance

Reye's Syndrome
A - Aspirin
V - Viral illness

C - Children under 12, confusion, combativeness, coma
R - Reflexes weak, respiratory failure, rigidity
　　Acute hepatic encephalopathy with increased liver function tests (LFT), ammonia, PT/PTT
　　Fragile X - large testicles, mental retardation (MR), normal or big head, X breaks when deprived of folic acid.

Fetal Alcohol - hypoglycemia, decrease growth, MR, cardiac abnormalities, ptosis.

Immunology

IgG is only immunoglobulin that crosses the placenta, affords infant 6 months of protection then mother's IgG is out of the system.

Bruton's X-linked hypogammaglobulinemia - missing B cells, susceptible to encapsulated bacteria (hemophilus, niserria, streptococcus), symptomatology begins after 6 months when mother's IgG goes away. Tx. pooled human gamma globulin.

DiGeorge Syndrome - third fourth pharyngeal pouch malformation, hypothyroidism so they are susceptible to tetany, cardiovascular abnormalities, lack thymus so no T cell differentiation, susceptible to viral and fungal infection. Tx. thyme transplant.

Wiskott Aldrich Syndrome
Deficit in T cell immunity
P - Pyogenic infection
E - Eczema
T - Thrombocytopenia

Ataxia-telangiectasia - decrease IgA, dilatation of small blood vessels in the sclera, repeated sinopulmonary infections.

Chronic Granulomatous Disease - X-linked recessive disorder, defective killing by neutrophils, susceptible to granulomas.

Immunity Reactions

Type 1 - immediate hypersensitivity IgE - urticaria, anaphylaxis
　　　　i.e. - pollen

Type 2 - complement mediated - antibody attack, IgG or IgM
     i.e. - Graves, Goodpasture
Type 3 - immune complex deposition
     i.e. - lupus
Type 4 - delayed hypersensitivity - T cell dependent, no antibody or
     complement
     i.e. contact dermatitis

Infectious Disease

Exanthems - rashes that arise as cutaneuous manifestations of infectious disease.

Roseola Infantum - exanthem subitum - sudden onset of fever 103-106, one to five days' duration, fever of unknown origin (FUO), maculopapular rash appearance on the trunk and spreads peripherally. Tx. supportive.

Mucutaneous Lymph Node Syndrome (Kawasaki) - strawberry tongue, lymphadenopathy, cracked lips, peeling of skin on finger and toe tips.

Erythema Infectuosum - fifth disease - children look like they have slapped cheeks - maculopapular rash on trunk and legs, pruritis.

Rubeola (measles) - highly contagious, paramyxoma virus, incubation eight to 12 days, then fever, cough, coryza, conjunctivitis; two days Koplik spots in mouth appear, and then two days later a maculopapular rash starts on the head. Tx. supportive.

Rubeola linked with subacute sclerosing panencephalitis (SSPE) happens months to years after the initial measles attack.

Scarlet fever - fever, pharyngitis, erythematous rash, caused by group A beta hemolytic strept, rash is finely punctuated spots that blanch with pressure, sandpaper skin, strawberry tongue. Tx. penicillin.

Common Infections

Rocky Mountain Spotted Fever - fever, headache, myalgia, caused by rickettsiia rickettsiia and transmitted by ticks, rose-colored blanching macules. Tx. chloramphenicol and tetracycline.

Chlymadia Trachomatis - neonatal conjunctivitis (purulent), pnuemonitis, eosinophilia, afebrile, caused by mother's vaginal secretions. Tx.- erythromycin.

Whooping Cough - bordetella pertusis, usually occurs in children younger than 2 years old, 2 week prodrome of upper respiratory infection (URI) with thick mucus, 2 week paroxysmal machine gun-like cough, stridourus inspiratory gasp, lymphocytosis, isolate organism with culture or immunoflourescence. Tx. erythromycin prevents transmission; you can quarantine to decrease spread.

Honey - can cause infection with botulism.

Meningicoccal Mengititis - if there is a local outbreak, administer quadravalent polysaccharide vaccine to those people who live in the area and are not infected.

H. Flu Meningitis - give rifampin prophylaxis to other people in the home if the infected child is younger than 4 years of age

Viral Croup - affects children age 6 months to 3 years ; parainfluenza, low fever, barking cough, inflammation of subglottic region, have hypercapnia. Tx. oxygen, humidification, epinephrine has transient effects, steroids in severe cases; do not give antihistamines or bronchodilators.

Epiglottitis - highest incidence ages 2 to 5 years; H. Flu type b most common pathogen, inflammation of epiglottis that can cause sudden respiratory obstruction. Lateral X-ray will show enlargement of epiglottis, high fever. Tx. ampicillin or chloramphenicol, nasotracheal intubation.

Otitis Media - most often caused by H. Flu and Strept. Tx. amoxocillin.

Orbital Cellulitis - number one cause of proptosis in children, caused most often by direct extension from infected ethmoid sinuses or skin infections.

Bacterial Meningitis (for this mnemonic think that children with meningitis can't touch their chins to their chest)
C - Coli, newborns usually affected by E. Coli
H - H. flu, 1- to 2-year-olds
N - Nieserria, 2- to 6-year olds
S - Strept, 6 and older
Lumbar puncture shows increase in protein and neutrophils, decrease in glucose positive kernig and brudzinski sign; when bacterial meningitis is suspected, administration of antibiotics should not await the results of diagnostic tests; usually can treat with a third generation cephalosporin.

Encephalitis - mostly viruses, HSV, arbo, entero.

Phakomatoses

Nuerofibromatosis type 1
1: 3000, chromosome 17, autosomal dominant
present with cafe au lait spots and benign harmartomas
harmartomas can become fibrosarcomas
development of neoplasms of the nervous system

Tuberous Sclerosis
rare, multiple harmatomas (tubers on the face)
MR and epilepsy
Shagren patches on buttocks

Von Hippel Landau
multiple hemangiomas in retina and brain
neoplasm in cerebellum
cysts in the kidney and pancreas

Sturge Weber Syndrome
rare, port wine stain of face

venous malformation involving the ipsalateral cerebral angioma

First three phakomatoses autosomal dominant - SWS not transmitted genetically.

Choanal Atresia - bony septum between nose and pharynx is missing, apneic, cyanotic which is relieved when crying because most infants' nose breathers except when they cry. Tx. surgery

Tetralogy of Fallot
most common cyanotic congenital cardiac anomaly
V - Ventricular septal defect
H - Hypertrophy - right sided
O - Overriding aorta
P - Pulmonary stenosis

Cystic Fibrosis - 1/2000, rare in blacks; diagnosis is made by sweat sodium level which will be increased, viscus lung secretions, pancreatic and hepatitic problems.

Congenital Displacement of the Hip
1/1000 occurrence, more common in girls
B - Barlow sign
O - Ortolani sign
G - Galeazzi sign (knees and hip flexed affected knee lower)
S - Shentons line - on X-ray imaginary curved line is broken

Failure to Thrive - TORCH
(Mother passes the disease to child like passing a torch)

T - Toxoplasmosis - hydrocephalus, cerebral calcification, chorioretinitis, transmitted by cat feces and raw meat.
O - Other like syphilis - skin rash, abortions, saddle nose, teeth (Hutchinson's notched incisor, screwdriver teeth, mulberry molars), oral lesions, bone lesions, anemia, saber shins.
R - Rubella - cataracts, deafness, congenital heart disease, MR.
C - CMV - MR, hearing loss, most common of the torch infections.
H - Herpes - 80 percent mortality

Rheumatic Fever — Strept Pyogenes, URI, strept throat, highest incidence ages 3 to adolescence; antigenic cross reaction between heart and strept - think SAFER CASES for minor and major criteria. Tx. Pen G, steroids, sedatives.

Minor Criteria
S - Strept group infection
A - Arthralgia
F - Fever
E - ESR elevated, ECG elongated PR interval
R - Rheumatic fever before

Major Criteria
C - Carditis
A - Arthritis - poly
S - Sydenhams chorea
E - Erythema marginatum
S - Subcutaneous nodules

VACCINATIONS

DPT - Diphtheria, Pertussis, Tetanus ; bacterial; D killed bacteria, P and T are toxoid; give at 2 months, 4 months, 6 months, 15 to 18 months, 4 to 6 years.

OPV - Oral Poliovirus — live attenuated, give at 2 months, 4 months, 15 to 18 months, 4 to 6 years.

MMR - Measles, Mumps, Rubella — live attenuated — 15 to 18 months.

Hib - H. influenza - bacterial - portion of the bacteria - 24 months.

TD - Tetanus and Diphtheria — 14 to 16 years, then every 10 years.

Don't give vaccination when there is acute fever, immunosuppression, transfusion, prior allergic reaction, change in neurologic status or convulsions.

No pertussis if they have a reaction at first injection, you can get postimmunization encephalomyelitis.

Live oral polio vaccine can give you paralytic poliomyelitis.

Herd immunity means not everyone has to be inoculated to prevent epidemics.

PEDS POTPOURRI

Child Abuse - retinoscopic exam shows retinal hemorrhages

Secondary Hypertension - think renal in kids

Lead Poisoning- mental retardation, check free erythrocyte proto-porphyrin levels. Tx. EDTA.

Five common causes of abdominal pain in children:
Lead poisoning
Appendicitis
Ileocecal intussception
Umbilical hernia
Mesenteric adenitis

Number one cause of death in infants is congenital anomalies.
Number two cause of death in infants is Sudden Infant Death Syndrome (SIDS)
Risk factors for SIDS: low socio-economic status (SES), boys, low birth weight.

Adrenogenital Syndrome - ambiquous genitalia, missing 21 hydrox-lyase, no production of aldosterone or cortisol; it is all shunted to the formation of androgens.

Jaundice — overflow of bilirubin, conjugation takes place in the liver.
Obstructive - no color in feces or urine.
Hepatitic - no color in feces or urine.
Hemolytic - color in both feces and urine.

Neonatal Jaundice - occurs in 50 percent of all newborns.
Non-physiologic - caused by: 1) unconjugated bilirubin, 2) delayed activity of glucoronyl transferase, 3) increase in bilirubin load, 4) decreased clearance from plasma, 5) higher bilirubin loads in preterm babies and breast fed babies.
Physiologic -1) hemolytic disease of the newborn, 2) ABO and Rh incompatibility, 3) RBC diseases, 4) Crigler Najjar, 5) Gilberts.

Congenital Lobar Emphysema - unilateral lobar hyperinflation, normal alveolar histology.

Retrolental Fibroplasia or Retinopathy of Prematurity - abnormal vasoproliferation in the retina, less than 1250g or less than 28 weeks very vulnerable; excessive oxygen increases risk, but no safe level known.

Hyaline Membrane Disease - premature birth, deficiency in pulmonary surfactant which leads to atelectasis; risk factors include males, cesarean, gestational diabetes. Tx. oxygen, intratracheal surfactant; prevent with corticosteroids.

Scabies - affects wrist and fingers, papular rash. Tx. lindane or malathion.

Peds Diarrhea, think celiac disease = gluten insensitivity; child fails to thrive, passes pale, malodorous, bulky stools, will have pot belly and wasted buttocks, definitive diagnosis made with jejunal biopsy will show blunt villi.

Intussusception - high incidence in 2 months to 2 year age group; number one cause hypertrophy of peyer patch or mesenteric nodes; other causes include meckel's diverticulum, polyp, lymphoma, foreign body; ileocolic, irritability, colicky pain, vomiting, current jelly stools, 50 percent, you can a feel sausage-shaped mass, empty right lower quadrant; barium enema shows coiled spring appearance. Tx. hydrostatic reduction by barium enema 15 percent recurrence rate.

Minimal Change Nephrotic Syndrome - proteinuria, hypoalbuminemia, hypercholestrolemia, 1 to 6 years of age, 90 to 95 percent respond to steroids; makes up 80 percent of all nephrotic syndromes in children; present with edema; acute infections can cause relapses.

Pyloric Stenosis - hypertrophy of smooth muscles of antrum, 15 percent familial, males more than females, vomitus is not bile stained, vomiting at second and third week, child hungry, loss of chloride and hydrogen ions due to vomiting.

OBSTETRICS AND GYNECOLOGY

Obstetrics
Labs of Pregnancy
Hemoglobin - decreased
Hematocrit - decreased
Total erythrocyte volume - increased
Serum iron - decreased
Clotting factors except for IX, XII - increased

Fasting blood glucose - increased
Sodium, potassium, bicarbonate - decreased
BUN - decreased but increases during term
WBC - increased
Alkaline phosphatase - increased
LDH, GOT, GPT - unchanged
Renal Flow - increased
Blood Pressure - unchanged
Heart Rate - increased

Urinary Tract Infection (UTI) in pregnancy - caused by hormonal dilation and ureteral hypoperistalsis as well as pressure from the pregnant uterus against the ureters, asymptomatic bacteruria occurs in 15 percent of all pregnancies and can progress to pyelonephritis. UTI is associated with increased risk of preterm labor and premature rupture of the membranes (PROM). Proof of cure cultures are required.

Human Placental Lactogen (HPL) - also called human chorionic somatomammotrophin (HCS), secreted by the syncytiotrophoblast and is similar to growth hormone, has no effects on lactation, has anti-insulin effect, causes lipolysis, low levels of HPL and estrogen suggest fetal growth retardation, can be used as a marker for trophoblastic tumors.

Diabetes in Pregnancy - occurs in 2 percent of pregnancy, HPL acts as anti-insulin, glucose rich urine excellent for bacteria growth so there is an increased chance of UTI, increased incidence of preeclampsia, cardiac and limb abnormalities, macrosomia 4500 gm, neonatal hypoglycemia, polyhydramnios which increases risk of abruptio placentae, preterm labor, and postpartum uterine atony. If no risk factors for diabetes at 24 to 28 weeks, perform one-hour glucola test. If it is over 140 mg percent plasma glucose, then three-hour glucose test with cut off values fasting 105 mg, one hour 190 mg, two hour 165 mg, three hour 145 mg; if two or more are high, then that patient has diabetes that needs to be controlled. Note glucose does cross the placenta but insulin does not. These patients can get Diabetic Ketoacidosis (DKA) which can cause fetal death so electronic fetal monitoring is required.

Ectopic Pregnancy - risk factors are prior tubal ligation, salpingitis (the number one risk factor), tubal repair, IUD, prior ectopic, increased age, black, Hispanic, 1/200 pregnancies are ectopic - 78 percent of ectopics are ampullary. Patients. have cervical motion tenderness (CMT), irregular bleeding or amenorrhea. Quantitative B-HCG levels can be followed at two-day intervals; early in pregnancy, levels should increase by at least 66 percent in 48 hours. Pelvic ultrasonography can identify an intrauterine pregnancy; serum progesterone less than 5.0 ng/ml indicates a nonviable pregnancy.

Incompetent Cervix - expulsion of fetus without labor; risk factors include cervical trauma, DES. Tx. Shirodkar cerclage.

Achondroplasia - in fetus test with ultrasound, autosomal dominant inheritance, failure of cartilage proliferation, short limbs normal face and trunk.

Open Meningomyeloceole - fetus secretes AFP so you can make the diagnosis by amniocentsis.

Postpartum Hemmorhage - most common cause is uterine atony; risk factors include hydramnios, twins, abnormal labor (preciptous, prolonged). Tx. includes oxytocin, but it can cause hypotension, uterine massage, methergine and PGE2; if hemmorhage still not controlled, then ligation of the hypogastric or uterine art.

Cesarean Section - increased mortality, must ligate the inferior epigastric artery before section.

Placenta Acreta - abnormal adherence of the placenta.

Placenta Previa - placenta at cervical opening.

Magnesium Sulfate - prophylaxis for preeclampsia seizures.

Metritis - most common infection postpartum, symptoms include fever and uterine tenderness, can give prophylactic antibiotics after Cesarean section.

Breech - can deliver vaginally if less than 3500 gms and more than 35 weeks.

HELLP Syndrome - hemolysis, liver dysfunction, low platelets; risk factors include multiparous and older women; patients. present with slight HTN, RUQ pain; high mortality associated with HELLP syndrome.

Tx. cardiovascular stabilization, delivery, correct coagulation abnormalities.

Herpes Genitalis (HSV2) - Cesarean section if active lesions 2 weeks before delivery. Neonate can get encephalitis. Patient should get yearly pap smears; no sex for one week after lesion; no acyclovir during pregnancy.

Rh negative mom - Rh negative dad — do nothing.

Rh negative mom - Rh positive dad or unknown — give Rhogam at 28 weeks if possible; if not at 28 weeks, then give within three days of delivery.

Magnesium Sulfate - tocolytic, does not cause increase in glucose; ritodrine, ethanol, terbutaline cause increase in glucose.

Preeclampsia - HTN see elevation of kidney and liver, could also get DIC; before 20 weeks it is hydatiform mole; with seizures - eclampsia.

Chadwick's Sign - bluish tint taken on by the vaginal mucosa in early pregnancy.

Fetal Complications of Antibiotics
Chloramphenicol - gray baby syndrome
Streptomycin - sensorineural hearing loss
Tetracycline - inhibition of teeth and bone
Sulfur Drugs - Kernicterus (increase free bilirubin)

Hyditaform Mole - preeclampsia in the first 20 weeks gestation, see snowstorm pattern on ultrasound, positive pregnancy test, painless bleeding, high HCG indicates increase chance in tumor later; follow HCG levels, malignant transformation choriocarcinoma 10 percent, highly sensitive to chemotherapy methotrexate.

Milestones
Fundus above pubic symphysis at 14 weeks.
Fundus at umbilicus 20 weeks.
Fundus at xiphoid process 38 weeks.
Fetal movements at 16 to 18 weeks quickening.

Labor - normally 37th to 42nd week, contractions at fundus with cervical effacement and dilation (lightening = abdomen changes shape, "baby dropping"), mother has an easier time breathing, bloody show, contractions every five minutes for at least one hour; Stage 1 is divided into latent which equals less than 4 cm. of dilation, active equals more than 4 cm. dilation.

Braxton Hicks - false labor, shorter in duration, resolves with ambulation.

Pitocin - causes increased contraction of the womb, 1/2 life of three to five minutes; continuous infusion IV.

Adverse Side Effects of Oxytocin - hypotension, uterine tetany, water intoxication, fetal distress.

Heparin doesn't cross the placenta so it is safe to give; warfarin does cross the placenta and causes fetal anomalies ; steroids cross and can cause cleft palate.

Arias Stella Reaction - confirms villi in endometrium; if not found ectopic pregnancy should be suspected.

Potter's Syndrome - fetal kidney excretes urine into amniotic fluid; fetal oliguria results in oligohydramnios which is associated with pulmonary hypoplasia (lungs need to inhale and exhale amniotic fluid to develop), renal agensis, flat nose, recessed chin, low-set ears.

Agalactiae - infants exposed from lower genital tract, one to four births, meningitis, septicemia, pnuemonia, more in premature, culture of cervix not that helpful, PROM or prematurity give antibiotics as emperic. Tx. postpartum endometritis.

PROM - 10 to 15 percent of births; associated with chorioamniotis, prolapsed umbilical cord, abruptio placenta; send fluid for phosphatidylglycerol to test for lung maturity; no interdigital exam so you decrease infection; if infection give antibiotics and deliver - do not inhibit labor; at 25 to 26 weeks, get pulmonary hypoplasia and band syndrome; if there is chorioamniotis, the mother will have fever, uterine tenderness, tachycardia. To test for amniotic fluid you can do the "fern" or Nitrazine test. Women with STDs have a higher incidence of PROM.

CANCERS IN WOMEN

Breast Cancer - most common cause of death in women in their 40s; second overall cause in death to lung cancer; first in incidence.

Fibrocystic Change -1/3 to 1/2 premenopausal women, symptomatic in half - caused by exaggerated response to hormones in the reproductive years or during hormone replacement, cyclic, bilateral pain and engorgement with diffuse bilateral nodularity.

Fibroadenoma - second most common breast tumor; affects young women; firm and painless, freely movable breast masses average 2 to 3 cm. in diameter; multiple 15 percent of time; these masses do not change during cycle.

Intraductal Papilloma - benign, not palpable; spontaneous bloody, serous, cloudy nipple discharge.

Mammary Duct Ectasia - affects women in their fifth decade; thick gray to black nipple discharge, itching.

Galactoceles - happens during lactation; cystic dilations, milky secretions.

More on Breast Cancer

Incidence increases with age, 85 percent occur after age 40; flattened and rubbery mass. The recommendations for women are:

Baseline mammography study for normal risk patients is between ages 35 and 40 then every one to two years from age 40 to 49, then annually from age 50. Ninety percent of breast cancers are found by the patient so self examination must be emphasized.

Mammography reduces rate of mortality by 30 percent. Mammography can pick up lesions that are 1 mm. in size. Palpable lesions are usually 1 cm. in size.

Vulvar Carcinoma - 90 percent are squamous cell variety, most commonly affects women age 65 to 70; patient often complains of vulvar pruritis.

Uterine Leiomyomas - affects 30 percent of all women; hormonally responsive tumors (estrogen), 1 percent go on to leiomyosarcoma.

Bleeding is the most common presenting sign, pelvic pressure and pain. Most do not require surgery.

Endometrial Cancer - risk factors include diabetes, obesity, increased age, low parity, infertile; presenting sign is post menopausal bleeding.

Cervical Cancer - risk factors include high parity, increase in partners, HPV 16 and 18; screening by pap smear has reduced the frequency of invasive cancer, presenting sign post coital bleeding.

Ovarian Carcinoma - high mortality; present with ascites, fifth most common cancer in women, third most common gynecological cancer; asymptomatic until metastasis, occurs usually in the fifth and sixth decade, whites more than blacks, risk increases with age, low parity, decreased fertility, delayed child bearing, long term ovulation protective (oral contraceptives protective), metastizes by direct extension just like cervical, Ca 125 possible tumor marker, mucinous cystadenocarcinoma (mucinous ascites) called pseudomyxomatous peritonei.

Most common ovarian tumor is benign cystic teratoma, also called dermoid cyst; called stroma ovari dermoid when it has functional thyroid tissue, 20 percent are bilateral.

Sertoli-Leydig Cell Tumors - stromal cell tumor of the ovary, secretes testosterone; produce male features, i.e. hirsutism.

Granulosa Theca Cell Tumor - stromal cell tumor of the ovary, secretes estrogen; produces female characteristics.

Miegs Syndrome - ovarian fibroma, ascites, right unilateral hydrothorax; does not secrete sex steroids.

GYNECOLOGY

Toxic Shock Syndrome - caused by Staph. Aureus, vaginal colonization, increased risk with tampon; symptoms include fever, hypotension, mucosal changes, desquamating rash. Tx. remove any foreign bodies, supportive care, B-lactamase resistant penicillin or cephalosporin.

Amenorrhea - causes include pregnancy, hypo-pit dysfunction, ovarian dysfunction, weight loss, marijuana, prolactin adenomas, injury. FSH and LH are usually low. If FSH and LH are high, then the ovary is not responding and patient experiences signs of estrogen deficiency such as hot flashes. Another cause could be Asherman's Syndrome which is scarring of uterus.

Dysfunctional Uterine Bleeding - state of chronic estrus - polycystic ovarian disease, exogenous obesity, adrenal hyperplasia - not regular ovulatory cycles, endometrial biopsy shows endometrial hyperplasia. Tx. give progesterone for 10 days and then give contraception.

Oral Contraceptives - suppress LH surge which inhibits ovulation thickens cervical mucus, decreases mobility of sperm, progestin effects cause atrophy of endometrium.

Infertility - one year without conception.
To induce ovulation, give gonadotropins FSH and LH, clomiphene, HCG.
Gardnerella Vaginitis - STD, thin white burning mild erythema, musty fishy odor, clue cells with KOH, positive whiff test, other bacteria can be found. Tx. metronidazole.

Trichamonis - 1/2 asymptomatic; itching, burning, copious, frothy discharge with rancid odor; dyspareunia and dysuria; strawberry petechiae. Tx. metronidazole.

Candida - not a STD, fungus that affects women during pregnancy, diabetes, obese, immunosuppressed, oral contraception, steroids, tight clothing; itching, bright red, adherent cottage cheese discharge, odorless — KOH see hyphae. Tx. miconazole —nystatin not as effective.

Fitz-Hugh-Curtis - gonococcal perihepatitis, RUQ pain, violin string adhesions around the liver.

Jarisch-Herxheimer - penicillin injection to someone with secondary syphilis; fever and chills.

Pelvic Relaxation (enterocele) - true hernia, small bowel pushing between rectum and vagina, low pelvic pain; caused by aging, trauma of childbirth, estrogen deficiency. Bladder wall moves into potential space of vagina causing stress incontinence (increased pressure in abdomen forces urine out).

Urethral Diverticulum - 3 Ds: dyspareunia, dysuria, dribbling.

Rokitansky-Kuster-Hauser Syndrome - uterus, cervix, vagina missing - patient still has puberty, breast growth, ovulation, but NO menstruation; associated with kidney problems, scoliosis. Tx. make artificial vagina.

Kallman's Syndrome - familial gonadotropin releasing hormone deficiency with hypoplasia of the olfactory; seen in men and women.

Mastalgia - Tx. Danazol (progesterone), vitamin E, methylxanthine.

Hirsutism - possible tumor in the ovary or adrenal gland, perform a radioimmunoassay for testosterone and dehyroepiandrosterone; measure PRL to see if tumor is in pituitary.

Estrogen Replacement Therapy - will decrease osteopenic fractures, vaginal dryness, hot flashes, improve sleep, protect from CV disease; unopposed estrogen will cause endometrial carcinoma and hyperplasia so give progestin to lower the risk; can't give estrogen if patient has breast cancer. Can give transdermal safely if patient has thromboembolic disease.

Estrogen and Birth Control Pills - can give to someone who had eclampsia, contraindications include HTN, abnormal liver function, sickle cell anemia, and malignant melanoma.

Gartner Duct Cyst - remnant of wollfian duct.

Uterus Anomalies - do IV pyelogram because of other anomalies associated with it.

Mastitis - lactating in one to three months, fever, malaise, general body ache becomes more localized days later, 90 percent unilateral, S. Aureus from babies pharynx, pen resist.; give diclox.

INTERNAL MEDICINE

This is the broadest of all of the core clerkships. During your clerkship, it will seem that you're expected to know a little bit about everything. In the exam there is a base of knowledge that is always tested so you should have a thorough understanding of these topics. In studying for the clerkship exam and boards for internal medicine, I find it beneficial to be able to jump from one topic to the next easily in the manner that you will be tested.

Glycosylated Hb A1c binds to glucose irreversibly, lasts the life of the blood cell (two months), use to measure glucose control in diabetics.

Ulcerative Colitis - colon inflammation, bloody diarrhea, leads to carcinoma 10 percent of the time, arthritis, toxic megacolon. For diagnosis you can do flex sigmoidoscopy, barium enema; be careful as it could cause a perforation. Lesions are continuos with no skip lesions. Tx. sulfsalzine (antibiotic and salicylate for inflammation), steroids, surgery.

Dissacharide Intolerance - you can do a hydrogen breath test following oral challenge.

Adult Respiratory Distress Syndrome - hypoxic failure, wet lung, increase in extravascular lung water; causes include DIC, bacterial septicemia, trauma, transfusion, pancreatitis, smoke inhalation, heroin overdose. Pathogenesis is an insult to capillary epithelium or alveolar endothelium extravasation. There will be extreme ventilation perfusion mismatch, tachypnea, dyspnea, rales, bilateral fluffy infiltrates on X-ray. Tx. 60 to 80 mmHg measured mixed venous oxygen content (CvO2) and mechanical ventilation with positive end-expiratory pressure (PEEP) which keep alveoli open and increase functional residual capacity.

Hemodialysis for Chronic Renal Failure - these patients fail to excrete phosphate (hyperphosphatemia), can't synthesize vitamin D; decrease intestinal absorption of Ca, decrease deposition in bone, hypocalcemia. This is a renal osteodystrophy due to secondary parathyroidism.

Hypothermia - patients will have tachycardia, ventricular fib., depression of CNS.

Zinc Deficiency - in cirrhosis, alcoholism, poor nutrition, pancreatic insufficiency, patients have an impaired sense of taste and smell, hyperpigmentation, night blindness.

Carbon Monoxide Poisoning - CO has increased affinity for hemoglobulin. Tx. give oxygen.

Pyelonephritis - commonly affects young females age 20 to 35; fever, flank pain, CVA tenderness, positive urine culture for bacteria (most common being E. Coli); there will also be WBC casts in the urine.

Urinary Obstruction - caused by stones or tumors; there will be hydronephrosis on abdominal ultrasound.

Acute Tubular Necrosis - causes include hypotension, toxins, ionic contrast, kidney shutdown, creatinine over 1.5 causes renal failure.

Menetrier's Disease - hypertrophic gastritis, rugal hypertrophy, males over 40, reduced or normal acid, overproduction of mucus causes increased protein loss.

Crohn's Disease - lesions are at the ileum with skip areas; less chance of cancer than Ulcerative Colitis; graunulomas, cobblestoning, string sign shows strictured lumen. Extraintestinal manifestations - arthritis and uveitis.

Decrease HDL, increase risk of CAD.

Reduction in cholesterol decreases the risk of CAD.

Kidney Stones - calcium oxalate is the most common stone and can be seen on plain film 90 percent of the time. Tx. lithotripsy.
Struvite stone caused by UTI with urea splitting bacteria (proteus).
Urate stone - radiolucent, caused by increase in uric acid. Seen in gout.
Cysteine stone - radiolucent, caused by cystinuria.

Thromboangitis Obliterans (Buerger's) - inflammation of artery, nerve, vein; causes thrombosis of the artery, men 20 to 40 who smoke - migratory superficial phlebitis, Jews do not have a higher incidence as once thought.

Acrocyanosis - bluish, purple discoloration of hands and feet due to slow circulation.

Prostatic Carcinoma - 18 percent incidence, uncommon before 50 years of age; adenocarcinoma is the most common, metastasis to the bone. Stages: A = accidentally found; B = bound to gland; C = contained in pelvis; D = distant mets. Staging done with CT, acid phosphatase, X-ray, bone scan, exploration. Tx. diethylstilbestrol and lutenizing hormone (lupron), radiotherapy, chemotherapy (5FU), surgery.

Benign Prostatic Hyperplasia - diminished stream, nocturia, residual urine, increases chances for calculi, curbstone symptom, strangury (slow painful urine drop by drop), infection; TURP more effective than surgery.

Subacute endocarditis most commonly caused by strept viridans; can see it after dental procedures.

Acute endocarditis commonly caused by Staph Aureus and epidermidis, mitral valve commonly involved, fever and malaise.

Prosthetic valves can cause endocarditis, embolization, perivalvular leak, mechanical failure, hemmorhagic complications.

Ventricular Septal Defect - most common defect; left to right blood flow, harsh systolic murmur left sternal border, spontaneous closure.

Patent Ductus Arteriosus - there will be a continuous machinery murmur sound.

Coarctation of Aorta - secondary hypertension, headache and lower extremity claudication, rib notching, HTN caused by decreased blood flow to kidney, activates Renin Angiotensin system.

Renovascular Hypertension - atherosclerosis accounts for 80 percent, 20 percent fibrodysplasia in children and young women — right renal effected 85 percent of time.

Graves - number one cause of proptosis in adults. Tx. PTU and methimazole decreases TSIs but has side effects of agranulocytosis (no neutrophils) and aplastic crises. Another Tx. is radioactive I 131 but cannot be administered to pregnant or breast feeding women.

Type 1 - MEN 1 - Wermer's Syndrome - hyperthyroidism, pancreatic islet cell tumor, pituitary adenoma.
Type 2 - MEN 2 - Sipple's Syndrome - hyperparathyroidism, medullary thyroid carcinoma, pheochromocytoma.
Type 3 - MEN 3 - Sipple's without hyperparathyroidism.

Anemia
CARS r STIL FAB

Normocytic
C - Chronic disease
A - Aplastic anemia
R - Renal failure
S - Sickle cell anemia

Microcytic
S - Sideroblastic
T - Thalassemia
I - Iron deficiency anemia low ferritin, high TIBC
L - Lead basophilic stippling of RBCs

Macrocytic
F - Folate deficiency
A - Alcohol - liver disease
B - B12 deficiency, pernicious anemia lack intrinsic factor

Sickle Cell Anemia - 1/500 blacks, normo hemolytic anemia, can get avascular necrosis of metacarpal and metarsals which is called hand-foot syndrome; splenic sequestration of blood cells causes hypovolemic shock; impaired spleen causes susceptibility to infections by encapsulated organisms so administer penicillin prophylaxis and vaccination;

patients prone to getting osteomyletis with Staph and salmonella. Diagnosis is made with electrophoresis and reticulocyte count. Tx. keep patients well hydrated, well oxygenated.

Bromocriptine - lowers PRL, decreases tumor size of prolactinoma.

E. Coli - most common cause of traveler's diarrhea. Tx. supportive.

Campylobacter - most common cause of bacterial diarrhea. Tx. erythromycin.

Salmonella Typhi - lethargy, constipation, headache, rose spots upper abdomen, can live in gallbladder; can cause hepatosplenomegaly; diagnosis with a Bac/StoolCx. Tx. chlorampenicol.

Salmonella Enteritis - fever, diarrhea, crampy pain. Tx. supportive.

Shigella - remember the four Fs: fingers, flies, food, feces. Common infection at day-care nursery. There will be WBCs in stool. Tx. supportive, TMP/SMX, ampicillin.

Hepatitis

Hep A - transmission is fecal oral, no permanent pathological sequlae; infection lasts two to six weeks.

Hep B - transmission is parenterally, 10 percent of patients develop chronic disease; patients are in a persistent carrier state for one to six months. Linked with cirrhosis and hepatocellular carcinoma.

Non A Non B - transmission usually from blood transfusions; two week to six month course; 20 percent to 30 percent chronic disease.

Delta - needs hepatitis B to survive.

Testicular Carcinoma - most common cancer in men 15 to 35; risk factors include cryptochordism, hernias, atrophy, increase in tumor markers AFP and HCG are used to monitor progression, LDH measures extent of disease. Tx. inquinal orchiectomy regardless of type; seminomas use node radiation instead of dissection.

Pleural Effusion - exudative = protein to serum greater than 0.5, LDH value greater than 200 IU; caused by infection, malignancy, pulmonary embolism, tuberculosis, abdominal disease, collagen vascular disease, uremia, Dresseler's syndrome (pericarditis some time after MI due to autoimmune reaction), chylothorax, drug-induced. Transudative = do not meet criteria of exudative, caused by CHF, nephrotic syndrome, cirrhosis, Meig's syndrome (ovarian fibroma with effusion), and hydronephrosis.

Polymyositis - leukocyte mediated attack, proximal muscle weakness, inflammatory infiltrates on biopsy, with rash called dermatoyositis, heliotrope rash on the eyelid, can't raise from chair, comb hair, dysphagia because disease affects pharyngeal muscles.

Barrett's Esophagitis - esophageal columnar epithelium instead of squamous epithelium, secondary to reflux with stricture and increased risk of developing adenocarcinoma.

Liver and Ammonia - dietary protein and urea normal source of nitrogen but bleeding increases nitrogen in the intestine and bacteria convert it to ammonia. Ammonia goes to liver where it is converted to urea and sent to kidneys if there is too much then excreted into blood. So if hepatic failure or portal collaterals or surgical shunting get increase in ammonia (portal systemic encephalopathy), can use nonabsorbable antibiotics neomycin and kanamycin which decrease bacteria that turn nitrogen to ammonia. If patient has kidney problems then you can use chlorotetracycline. Another solution is lactulose - mild cathartic, bacteria make it into lactic acid and acetic acids decrease caloric pH which interferes with ammonia transfer across colonic mucosa.

Portal circulation takes nutrients absorbed from GI and processes them in the liver also detoxifies substances and rids blood of GI bacteria. Blood filters through sinusoids to central vein then to hepatic vein which goes to inf. Vena Cava.

Budd Chiari - endophlebitis of the hepatic veins; can cause ascites and cirrhosis.

Hyperthyroid - T4 T3 increased, T3 uptake increased, TSH decreased, TBG can be low or elevated.

Acute Pericarditis - can be caused by coxsackie type B virus, idiopathic most common cause in adults; symptoms include chest pain (sharp), friction rub.

Pericardial Effusion - Ewart's sign - rub or dullness at left lung base posteriorly due to compression of lung by pericardial sac; can be caused by pericarditis.

Cardiac Tamponade - can cause neck vein distention, hypotension, pulsus paradoxicus (fall in systolic blood pressure and pulse volume when patient breaths in - lung fills with air constricting heart even more).

Kussmaul's Sign - in restrictive pericarditis, increased neck vein distention with inspiration.

Tetracycline - can use for (CRAM) chylamidia, ricketsia, acne, mycoplasm.

Laennec's Cirrhosis - alcohol induced cirrhosis; ascites caused by decreased albumin and oncotic pressure; increase back pressure so you get transudative fluid in peritoneal cavity and increase aldosterone, eventually causing varices in the esophagus and hemorrhoids, encephalopathy, hepatorenal syndrome (increase renal vascular constriction, decrease blood flow).

Primary Biliary Cirrhosis - clinically same as Laennec's, happens to 40- to 60- year-old females, it is an autoimmune disorder; patients complain of pruritis.

Sterile Pyuria - think renal tuberculosis.

Pyelonephritis - E. Coli number one cause; patients get chills, fever, vomiting, flank pain, anorexia. Tx. IV cephalosporin and aminoglycoside.

If giving antibiotics and no effect on fever, think abscess.

Aspirin - most common drug poisoning; affects hepatic and renal - 100 mg/kg in blood is toxic, start emesis, give activated charcoal, alkalysing urine.

Acetometophan - Tx. give N-acetylcysteine which replenishes glutathione, decrease glutathione increases hepatotoxicity.

Alzheimer's - chronic dementia after 45; mimics depression; no genetics proven; pathologically you see nuerofibillary tangles, atrophy, cortical choline acetyltransferase decrease.

Systemic Hypertension - number one cause of CHF.
CHF low output - Tx. decrease Na+, give diuretic and digoxin.
CHF high output - decrease Na+, give diuretic.

Congestive Cardiomyopathy - dilated and poorly contractile ventricles; causes include familial, beri beri, postpartum, chagas disease. Tx. use vasodilators.

Hypertrophic Cardiomyopathy - hypertrophy of ventricular septum - systolic murmur of the left sternal border, S4. Tx. Beta blockers, slow heart rate and decrease obstruction, increase left ventricular filling size, decrease blood flow.

Restrictive Cardiomyopathy - non-compliant heart; causes include amyloidosis, hemachromatosis, sarcoidosis.

Myocarditis - can be caused by coxsackie B and other viruses.

MI - thrombosis or necrosis, unrelieved by nitro; initially see ST elevation, as ST falls prominent Q waves and T waves become inverted, subendocardial infarction ST depression, rise in MB-CK, SGOT, LDH 2/1 flips to 1/2, first 24 hours could have arrhythmias, inferior wall MI - RCA, SA, and AV node affected can get sinus bradycardia and AV node block; anterior wall MI - ADCA septum affected bundle branch block, CHF, MRS, cardiac rupture, left ventricular aneurysm. Tx. nitro for coronary spasm, morphine sulfate, prophylactic lidocaine, phenytoin, streptokinase, atropine or isoproterenol, Swanz-Ganz measures filling pressure less than 18 mmHg give volume, measure ejection fraction for left ventricle dysfunction under 40 percent increases mortality.

Migraine - visual aura with flashes, scintalating scotoma, throbbing unilateral temporal headache; caused by stress, fatigue, tyramine foods, phenylethamine in wine, chocolate - usually positive, family history. Tx. ergotamine tartrate, antiemetics, analgesia.

Tension Headache - bilateral, bandlike and viselike.

Transient Ischemic Attacks - monocular blindness, no headache.

Cranial Arteritis - painless, lose vision.

Guillain Barre Syndrome - postinfectious demyelinatig polyneuropathy, autoimmune, bilateral facial paralysis, respiratory difficulties, lower and upper extremity problem, sensory is intact.

ALS - degenerating corticospinal tracts, upper motor neuron paralysis, hypertonic.

Hashimoto's - goiter, hypothyroidism.

Chemotherapy and Side Effects

Methotrexate -megaloblastic changes in bone marrow; rescue with folinic acid
Cyclophosphamide - hemmorhagic cystis, bone depression
L-asparaginase - pancreatitis
Vinblastin - myelosuppression
Vincristin - nuerotoxocity
Daxorubicin - cardiomyopathy
Bleomycin - pulmonary fibrosis
Cisplatin - nephrotoxocity
Busulfan - adrenal insufficiency

Organophosphate - irreversible cholinesterase inhibitor; can cause cholinergic excess; give 2PAM (pralidoxine) to treat toxicity.

Myasthenia Gravis - anti-AcH receptor; Abs decrease receptors at the NMJ, patient will experience fatigue after repetition and will have increased thyroid trouble, 10 percent get thymoma, can get respiratory fatigue acidosis hyperventilation, CO_2 retention.

Eaton Lambert Syndrome - Abs to calcium channel in motor nerve decreases Ach release; seen in small cell carcinoma of the lung; increase muscle strength with exertion.

Clostridium Botulinum - interferes with calcium; repetitive stimulation increases response.

Goodpastures's - young males, hemoptysis and nephritis, anti-basement membrane antibodies.

Sarcoidosis - non-caseating granulomas, more common in blacks due to impaired immunity; 90 percent involvement in the lung causing restriction, bilateral hilar adenopathy and interstial infiltrate (bat wing appearance on X-ray); patients. can get uveitis, bell's palsy, arrythmias, skin involvement. Tx. steroids, most have regression in 2 years with no recurrence, but damage is permanent, serious complications develop in 25 percent of patients.

Wegener's Granulomatosis - glomerulonephritis and granuolomatous vasculitis of URT, rhinorrhea, multiple, bilateral nodal infiltrate that cavitate, effusions. Tx. predinisone and cyclophosphamide causes remission in 90 percent.

Bronchiectasis - productive cough; sputum layers out in three parts.

Rhuematoid Arthritis - polyarthritis hands and feet, pleurisy with or without effusion, Rhuematoid nodules in lungs, Rhuematoid. factor positive.

Scleroderma - lung fibrosis, pleura thickening, raynaud phenomenon, skin, GI, kidneys, heart effected, most often affects women, autoimmune disease, Abs to Scl.

Henoch Schloen Purpura - diffuse vasculitis and URI, purpura on buttocks, extensor surfaces of the legs and arms, patients develop arthritis, HAEMATURIA is seen in 70 percent of patients.

Interstitial Lung Disease - C- collagen vascular, cardiac problems
H - histiocytosis X
I - Infection, idiopathic
P - pnuemoconioses
S - silicosis, sarcoidosis

Anion Gap - Na+ - (Cl- + HCO3-) normal 10 to 14, it measures the amount of other anions in the system. Renal failure causes increase in sulfate, phosphate, and organic acids. Tissue hypoxia causes lactic acidosis (hypotension, shock, CHF, anemia). Other causes include diabetic Ketoacidosis. Methanol, salicylates, ethylene glycol, paraldehyde.

Idiopathic Thrombocytopenic Purpura - ITP autoimmune process after viral illness or after immunization, petechaie and ecchymosis, 80 percent resolve spont., can get DIC or hypersplenism. Tx. corticosteroids, gammaglobulins, splenectomy.

Acute Chest Pain - five killers; remember: MAPPE - myocardial infarction, aortic aneurysm, pulmonary embolism, pnuemothorax, esophageal bleed (Boerhaave's Syndrome - spontaneous post-emetic rupture, instrumentation, trauma, foreign body, suture line leak).

Parasympathetic ————> Ach ————> Ach Dominant in eye, heart, GI, Bladder, secretions
Sympathetic ————> Ach ————> NE B1= heart, B2 = lungs, @1 = peripheral vessels and GI, @2 = presynaptic inhibitory regulator

PSYCHIATRY

This section includes: psychiatry, population statistics and ethics. Don't be surprised when you see questions that you feel have nothing to do with psychiatry being asked in this section of the test.

Phenytoin (Dilantin) - used for grand mal seizures; toxicity causes nystagmus and also HAG - hirsutism, acne, gingival hyperplasia.

Acute Dystonic Reaction - oculogyric crisis, posturing, side effect of antipsychotics; caused by excessive stimulation of hypersensitive dopamine receptors; attacks subside spontaneously or can give anticholinergics or Diazepam.

Antidepressants - can cause cardiac depression, neurological disturbances.

Transient Global Amnesia - late middle age, fully alert, distant memory intact, can last several hours.

Psuedodementia - dementia syndrome of depression, elderly.

Schizoid - example: a lighthouse keeper.

Schizotypal - example: a bag lady.

Fugue - unaware of identity loss.

Antisocial - does not recognize the rights of others.

Suicide = hopelessness.

Tarasoff case - requires psychotherapist to warn potential victims of patient's expressed intent to harm.

Neuroleptic Malignant Syndrome - after antipsychotic use, patients get hypothermia with increased muscle tone, involuntary movements, renal and lung involvement; 25 percent fatal. Tx. supportive; also give Dantrolene and Bromocriptine.

Dementia - normal consciousness with decreased orientation, cognition, and memory.

Neologism - seen in manics and schizos , newly invented word or word used in a new way.

Verbigeration - repeating words, phrases, or sentences.

Echolalia - repetition of someone's speech.

Clang association - relationship of words based on sound; seen in mania.

Illusion - sensory misperception with a stimulus (long shadow looks like a monster).

Hallucination - sensory without any stimulus (hearing things).

Delusion - false idea (I am Napoleon).

Bipolar - give lithium; second line is carbamezepine.

Displacement - emotions, ideas, or wishes transferred from their original object, person, or situation to a more acceptable one. Common in phobias (Person was raped by a pilot and has a fear of flying).

Isolation - "effect" attached to idea rendered in unconscious, leaving conscious idea emotionally neutral; seen with Ob-compulsives (Baby killer has no expression during killings).

Reaction Formation - ideas, behaviors, effect, exact opposite of the one he or she harbors (Dates nuns when really wants to be with hookers).

Undoing - unacceptable act is symbolically acted out in reverse; relieves anxiety, guilt.

Higher level of education means more use of health care system.

Predictive value of test is related to prevalence. If you have a screening test that is checking for disease that is not found often, no matter how sensitive, the predictive value will be low.

Confounder - variables whose effects are entangled with other variables; must be related to disease and risk factors.

Chi square compares raw numbers.
T test compares means.

Suicide - risk increases at age 40 to 50; higher risk in males during adolescence and after age 45.
Males commit more suicide than females; females attempt more suicide; minorities (except for Native Americans) decrease in suicide rates; talking about it can serve as deterrent -eight out of 10 tell before they do. Moral of the story: Take people seriously.

ADHD - peak incidence 8 to 10 years old; remember: HII - hyperactivity, impulsivity, inattention; give methylphenidate (ritalin); later in life, patients can become antisocial.

Malingering - conscious, voluntary production of physical symptoms.

Conversion - unconscious-(I want to strike you; my hand is paralyzed.)

Sublimation - undesirable impulses are turned into acceptal behavior. This can become an obsession.

Projection - attributing unacceptable ideas to another. This can become paranoia.

Alcoholism - some signs are: impairment in social and occupational tasks, bingeing, inability to cut down, two or more blackouts, tolerance. Male children of alcoholic fathers have high predisposition.
Wernicke's - physical signs of thiamine deficiency: nystagmus, ataxia, confusion, confabulation, lethargy, ophthalmoloplegia.
Korsakoff's - mental signs of thiamine deficiency: psychosis, amnesia. Tx. AA; Al-non for Family; Insight; Disulfiram (Antabuse), which is acetylaldehyde dehyrogenase inhibitor; chlordiazepoxide, a sedative hypnotic; thiamine; folic acid; mag sulfate 1 gm. intramuscularly- protects against seizures; no antipsychotics as they can precipitate seizures. Alcohol and Benzo or barbiturate can be fatal (seizures and alcohol predispose to aspiration).

Blacks have increased risk of top 10 death patterns except suicide.

All minorities have less rate of suicide; Latinos and blacks increased rate of HIV.

Leading causes of death, all ages - heart, cancer, injuries.
Leading cause of infant death - congenital anomalies, SIDS, low birth weight.

Leading cause of death ages 1 to 14 - injuries, cancer, congenital anomalies.

Leading cause of death ages 15 to 24 - injuries, homicide, suicide.

Leading cause of death ages 25 to 64 - cancer, heart, injuries.

Sensitivity - TP/ TP+FN Specificity - TN/ TN+ FP

Null hypothesis = no difference in two groups.
P measures if the difference is by chance.
Type 1 error - rejecting the null hypothesis when it is true.
Type 2 error - not rejecting a false null hypothesis.

Relative Risk - RR= I exposed/I unexposed

mean, median, mode ———— average, middle, most

correlation coefficient- -1 to +1 0 means no relationship

Medicare does not cover routine physicals, eye/ear exam for glasses/hearing aid, immunizations, routine foot care, nursing home for more than 100 days total, custodial care, self administered medications.

Ten percent of elderly have dementia; 10 percent age 75 and over are in a nursing home, 20 percent over 85 years of age are in a nursing home.

Forty one percent of health care is paid by the government.

Most common principal diagnosis resulting in an office visit by males to a physician is essential HTN. For women, the most common reason is pregnancy.

1990: 72 divorces per 100 marriages.

Less marital satisfaction for people with children.

Single predictor for suicide is helplessness.

SES - occupation and education, income is not a direct determinant.

Low SES - more sharply defined sex roles, more rigid expectations, prejudice, poor development of language skills, language-action oriented, most are single parent families.

Homeless - 1/2 to one million, more than half are non-white; large portion single women with children.

Fifty percent of pregnancies are unintended; 10 percent of teenage girls will become pregnant; pregnancy is the leading cause of female dropout from school; 80 percent of sexually active teenagers do not use birth control.

Top causes of death in 25 to 44 year old males: injury, AIDS, heart. Number one cause of death in black males is AIDS.

Number one way of contracting AIDS today is through IV drug use.

Number one STD is Gonorrhea.

Number one male cancer: prostate (incidence); lung (death).

Number one female cancer: breast (incidence); lung (death).

The most common birth control for married couples is sterilization.

The most likely source of violence for a woman is an ex-spouse or boyfriend.

Greatest single problem associated with infant mortality is low birth weight: white 7.6; black 18; Hispanic 10.3.

Infant Doe Case - foregoing lifesaving surgery for neonate with Down's and TE fistula.

SURGERY

Musculoskeletal problems

Scoliosis - patients have asymmetric shoulder levels, found in 3 to 5 percent of women adolescents.

Slipped Caput Femoral Epiphysis (SCFE) - displaced femoral head seen most often in obese males.

Osteochondritis Dissecans - bone pulls from cartilage at femoral condyle.

Rhuematoid Arthritis (RA)- usually affects middle age females, symmetrical, affects hands first then lower extremities, cervical spine, affects PIP joints, osteopenic hip and knee problems, RA nodules in the elbow; called Felty's when there is splenic enlargement; called Still's in adolescents; Caplin Rheumatiod Pneumoconioses when there is RA and silica exposure. Common in coal miners or people who work with ceramic or cement.

Degenerative Joint Disease - commonly affects distal interphelangeal joint.

Ankylosing Sponylitis - young men 15 to 30 years of age, complain of worsening back pain, rheumatoid factor negative, starts at sacroiliac and works way up the back, fused facet joints, increased risk of fractures, HLA B-27 positive, intercostal joint problems, upper pulmonary lobe fibrosis.

Colles Fracture - dorsoradio displaced fx of the distal radial metaphysis with associated fx of ulnar styloid, dinner fork, Chinese finger traps.

Scaphoid Fx - fx not seen initially on X-ray; high incidence of AVN.

Thyroglossal Cyst or Fistula - in fetal development, thyroid tracts from foremen cecum past hyoid; remnant of this migration is a cyst or fistula which appears as a midline mass anterior of neck. Tx. surgical removal.

Branchial Cleft Cyst, Sinus, Fistula - first and second Branchial cleft - first cleft is close to facial nerve so disruption here causes problems from ext. auditory canal to the submandibular region; second cleft is close to the hypoglossal nerve so disruption here causes problems from tonsil to the sternocliedomastoid.

Zenker's Pharyngeoesophageal Junction - acquired diverticula, patients get airway contamination, aspiration, regurgitation.

Heparin - effective in DVT, arterial emboli, PE, but not effective after hip surgery.

Halothane - side effect: patients can get Malignant Hyperthermia; 60 percent mortality, incidence is 1:35,000; Halothane can also cause postop hepatitis with 50 percent mortality.

Cardiac Angiography - can cause acute tubular necrosis, nonionic contrast less sequlae than ionic contrast.

B12 absorbed in the ileum with intrinsic factor which is secreted in the stomach, deficiency causes pernicious anemia (macrocyctic), neurologic symptoms, atrophic glossitis. Do Schilling test for intrinsic factor; this is a complication of gastric surgery.

Duodenal Ulcer - due to an increase in acid, pain relieved by food; three times more common than gastric ulcer; risk factors include increasing age, men, smoking, aspirin, NSAID, alcohol, hereditary, blood group O. Patients get anemia from chronic blood loss. There is an association with RA, COPD, cirrhosis, renal disease.

Gastric Ulcer - decrease in mucus in stomach; aggravated by food, weight loss; rule out malignant process which is seen 5 percent of the time; absence of acid speaks more for malignancy.

Therapy for DU and GU - intensive antacids, calcium containing acids stimulate gastric release; side effect: diarrhea; cimetidine, ranitidine (more potent, less p450), sucralfate coats the ulcer. Bland diet not a factor but patient must stay away from alcohol, milk, caffeine (all promote acid). Surgery consists of subtotal gastrectomy or vagotomy.

Cholecystitis and Cholangitis - inflammation of gallbladder and biliary tree. Patients with cholangitis infection have Charcot's Triad (RUQ pain, high fever with shaking chills, jaundice); also can have leukocytosis; increase bilirubin and alk phos.

Most common tracheoesophageal fistula: 86 percent - esophageal atresia, with distal esophagus connected to the trachea; 40 percent have other malformations. VATER - vertebral and anal, tracheoesophageal fistula, radial limb dysplasia or renal anomalies. Present in infants in respiratory distress, salivating and drooling; X-ray shows gas free abdomen.

Chronic Pancreatitis - 90 percent alcohol related, caused by cystic fibrosis in children. Patients present with pain, steatorrhea, weight loss, jaundice, and diabetes. You see calcifications on X-ray, ERCP shows chain of lakes sign.

Most common pancreas malignancy: adenocarcinoma; more common in men. Risk factors include hereditary pancreatitis, smokers, diabetics, maybe coffee. Pain relieved by sitting up and bending both knees, positive courvoisier sign (gallbladder palpable), 5 percent survival rate.

Roux en Y operation - jejunum to stomach, duodenum to jejunum.
Billroth 1 operation - antrectomy and vagotomy.
Billroth 2 operation- antrectomy and vagotomy, jejunum with duodenal pouch.

Dumping Syndrome - after gastric resection, patients get nausea, vomiting, crampy abdominal pain, diaphoresis. Contents are then dumped quickly into the small bowel. Tx. includes low carbo, high fat, high protein diet; anticholinergics seem to help.

Afferent Loop Syndrome - post prandial abdominal pain, relieved by bilious vomiting, patients get build up of biliary and pancreatic secretions; relief when discharged to stomach. Decrease this syndrome by avoidance of a long or twisted afferent limb and construction of a patent anastomosis after Billroth 2.

Tumor Markers
Prostatic cancer/Acid phosphatase
Calcitonin/Medullary thyroid carcinoma
CEA/Cancer of colon
Alpha fetoprotein/Hepatocelluar carcinoma
HCG/Hydatiform mole
LDH/Lymphoma

Heavy chains/Multiple myeloma

Juvenile polyps - no malignant potential, affects adults

Gigantism - acromegaly (pituitary adenoma), increase in growth hormone, GH has anti-insulin effect; produces diabetes, also possible hypertension.

Signs of Respiratory Failure - Respiratory Rate > 34/minute, cyanosis, Heart Rate > 120, Arrhythmias

Diverticulitis - left sided appendicitis, LLQ pain, leukocytosis. Tx. ampicillin, IV fluid, and NPO.

Post surgical pelvic abscess - think bacteroides fragilis.

ADH - water in Na+ out
Aldosterone - Na+ in, K+ out

Hypospadias - most common anomaly of the penis, urethral meatus on undersurface, ventral curvature, 10 percent of patients have undescented testis, foreskin will be used for reconstruction; determine genetic sex, order IVP because these patients have increased incidence of renal abnormalities.

Peritonitis - lie in bed supine, knees flexed, limit intercostal respirations since any motion intensifies abdominal pain.

Meckel's Diverticulum - persistence of omphalomesenteric duct; it is known as the disease of 2s: 2 percent of the population have one, it is usually 2 feet from ileocecal valve, 2 inches long. Patients can have pancreatic tissue or gastric mucosa, chronic blood loss, diverticulitis; can present as appendicitis; can cause volvulus or intussception.

Volvulus - in elderly, occurs in the sigmoid colon; in younger people, it is due to malrotation.

Ileostomy - performed with colonic resection; will cause cholethiasis, urolithiasis, sodium depletion, vitamin B12 depletion; most important item to remember: salt and water depletion.

ENT procedure complication - air embolism causing hypotension and cyanosis.

Orthopedic procedure complication - fat embolism.

Plummer Vinson - iron deficiency, dysphagia, esophageal web, more common in women.

Achalasia - disease causing denervation of esophagus, lower esophageal sphincter does not relax; histologically there is loss of ganglion cells in myenteric plexus patients can get megaesophagus; can be caused by Chagas disease; patients suffer from aspirations; 5 percent increase incidence of esophageal carcinoma.

Esophageal Cancer - 1 percent of GI cancer; 2 percent of cancer deaths; alcohol and cigarettes cause marked increased risk. Most of these cancers are squamous cell, most in the middle 50 percent of the esophagus; Barrett's metaplasia causes adenocarcinoma of the last third of esophagus.

Stomach cancer - adenocarcinoma most common. In Japan it is the most common malignancy; in the U.S. it is more common in the north, in the poor, and in blacks. Patients complain of fullness or pain after a large meal.

Medical Potpourri

Dr. Stanford Shulman, codirector of the microbiology laboratory at Chicago's Children's Memorial Hospital and Northwestern Pediatrician, reported a case of Salmonella to the Centers for Disease Control in Atlanta. All Salmonella cases must be reported to the state. It turned out that Dr. Shulman had discovered a new strain which he had to name. Dr. Shulman admired Michael Jordan's basketball ability so much that he decided to pay tribute to him. The name of the new strain of Salmonella is, Salmonella mjordan.

✚ ✚ ✚

One of the first HMOs was started in 1933 in the Mojave Desert for men building an aqueduct to carry fresh water across the desert from the Colorado River to Los Angeles. When workers were injured they had to travel across the desert to Los Angeles. The ambulance was described as a "oven on wheels." Dr. Sidney Garfield , a Los Angeles surgeon, decided to build a 10-bed hospital in the desert for the workers of the aqueduct. To avoid bankruptcy he convinced the worker's compensation insurance carriers to pay for some of the care given to the workers. He also had the construction contractor of the workers collect five cents a day by payroll deduction as prepayment for health care. The hospital moved into the black and paid for the construction of two more hospitals.

In 1938 Dr. Garfield was asked by Henry J. Kaiser to develop a similar program for the his workers at the Grand Coulee Dam in Washington.

❖ ❖ ❖

Dr. Garfield had a 75-bed hospital renovated and the pre-payment plan was offered to the workers and their families. The rate was 50 cents a week per worker and spouse, and 25 cents per child. Today, Kaiser Permanente is the nation's largest private health care program.

❖ ❖ ❖

The bacteria Salmonella Typhi can cause enteric fevers. Unlike other bacteria, it can live in the human digestive system without causing symptoms. It can be transmitted by feces and vomit. The best known story of an S. Typhi carrier was "Typhoid Mary" Mallon, a cook in New York who was known to have infected 53 people, killing five. She was also suspected of causing an outbreak in Ithaca, New York which infected 1,300. When authorities tried to apprehend her, she attacked them with her butcher's knife.

❖ ❖ ❖

A "quack" is an ignorant pretender of medical or surgical skill. The word is derived from the Dutch word quacksalver. People use to sell salves claiming that they could cure syphilis. These salve sellers use to boast about their cure rate. Some people began stating that these sellers use to quack about their salves. Hence the name quacksalver. Since they never cured anyone, quack became synonymous with a person who claimed extraordinary healing powers but produced no results.

Mesmerism was an actual medical movement started by Dr. Franz Anton Mesmer in 1773. Mesmerism included hypnotism, the identification of psychosomatic disorders, group therapy, and psychoanalysis. He claimed that the planets affected human health. He also placed magnets on patients' bodies to try to relieve pain, thus coining the phrase animal magnetism. He felt that the manipulation of animal magnetism could cure the sick.

In the 17th and 18th centuries, surgeons were paying for cadavers for dissection. The cadavers were sometimes provided by body snatchers who sometimes murdered people to attain cadavers. In 1823, William Burke and William Hare murdered 16 people and sold the cadavers to Dr. Robert Knox. They were finally apprehended. Dr. Knox was cleared. Hare turned in evidence and was released. Burke was prosecuted, hanged, tanned, and his body was used for a dissection demonstration.

The authors Chekhov, John Keats, Somerset Maugham, William Carlos Williams, Sir Arthur Conan Doyle, and Michael Crichton (the author of Jurassic Park), were all physicians.

In the Middle Ages, barbers were responsible for performing surgery. The red-and-white barber poles informed people that they performed surgery. The white of the pole symbolized bandages and the red symbolized blood.

In 1876, Lord Lister of England pioneered antiseptic techniques for surgery. Before that time, surgeons would operate in their streetclothes. Lord Lister's name is seen each day on the antiseptic Listerine.

In the early 1900s, women were not allowed to study medicine in England. The first woman to study medicine disguised herself as a man. Dr. James Barry kept the secret of her sex and the fact that she had a child until her death.

There are more women physicians than male physicians in Russia.

Carrion's Disease is caused by infection with the bacteria Bartonella Bacilliformis. The disease causes an acute febrile anemia and chronic cutaneous eruption. Carrion was a medical student who had a patient with a B. Bacilliformis infection. Afraid that he would contract the disease and become sick, he inoculated himself with the fluid from the cutaneous eruption. He contracted the disease from the inoculation and died.

Leaf cutter ants are used for suturing wounds in East Africa and Brazil. Edges of wounds are united. Then the ants are allowed to bite through the wound. Once the stitch is made the ant's body is cut.

What is a consultation? Oliver Wendell Holmes wrote this poem:

> Now when a doctor's patients are perplexed,
> A consultation comes in order next-
> You know what that is? In a certain place
> Meet certain doctors to discuss a case
> And other matters, such as weather,
>   crops,
> Potatoes, pumpkins, lager-beer, and
>   hops.
> For what's the use? - there's little to
>   be said,
> Nine times in ten your man's as good
>   as dead;
> At best a talk (the secret to disclose)
> Where three men guess and sometimes
>   one man knows.

You will hear many physicians telling you to treat the patient as a whole.

Take these words of wisdom from Plato (427 - 347 B.C.):

The cure of many diseases is unknown to the physicians of Hellas, because they are ignorant of the whole, which ought to be studied also; for the part can never be well unless the whole is well .... This ..... is the great error of our day in the treatment of the human body, that the physicians separate the soul from the body.

On August 17,1996, a 17-year-old man walked into an MCAT exam room demanding a test at gunpoint. The would-be robber was subdued by a proctor and angry students when he put his air pellet gun down to look over the test. The young man needed treatment at a local hospital for multiple injuries.

❖ ❖ ❖

The Nobel Prize was started by Alfred Bernhard Nobel (1833-1896) the inventor of dynamite. Mr. Nobel, troubled by the potentially destructive uses of his invention, used his fortune to reward human ingenuity for peaceful purposes. He left $9 million to establish a series of prizes in his name, including the Nobel Prize in Medicine and Physiology.

❖ ❖ ❖

The Tuskegee Syphilis Experiment was conducted by the Public Health Service from 1932 to 1972. The experiment was to study the natural course of syphilis if left untreated. A group of black men who contracted syphilis was the test group. These men became very ill due to the various effects of the syphilis. The controversy of this study has changed human research since its exposure in 1972. You can no longer withhold treatment for any reason when you know that the treatment is effective in curing the disease.

❖ ❖ ❖

The first stethoscope is attributed to Laennec. When a young lady, accompanied by her father, came to Laennec's office for a consultation, he had to listen to her heart sounds without causing a scandal. So he rolled up a piece of paper, placed one side on his ear and one side on her chest. The father was happy and Laennec made history.

Santiago Ramon Y Cajal the winner of the Nobel Prize in Medicine in 1906 tried two jobs before entering the medical profession. He served two apprenticeships, one in barbering and one in shoemaking. He failed them both and was forced to take up his father's trade - medicine.

❖ ❖ ❖

Native Americans were doing neurosurgery long before medicine was even a discipline. When their warriors would go to battle and have head injuries that would cause brain hemorrhages the tribe would know the symptoms and treat by cutting holes in the cranium to let the blood drain out. This was discovered by looking at the skulls from hundreds of years ago and identifying craniotomy sites.

❖ ❖ ❖

In 1300 B.C. the pregnant Egyptian women use to urinate on wheat and spelt. If the wheat grew then they knew she was going to have a boy. If the spelt grew they would predict a girl. If nothing grew then they thought that the woman would not bear. We now know that estrongenic hormones in urine can speed up germination processes in certain seeds and cuttings.

❖ ❖ ❖

A non-verified story has it that Charles II was dismayed by the growing number of royal bastards so he called his physician Dr. Condom who made the Kind a prophylactic that worked well enough to earn Dr. Condom a knighthood and a word in the dictionary.

About the Author

Rolando Stephen Toyos, M.D. received his bachelor of arts in biology from the University of California, at Berkeley. He then graduated with a master of arts in science education from Stanford University in Palo Alto, California. After receiving his master of arts, he taught high school biology at Sequoia High School in Redwood City, California. After a few years of teaching he went on to the University of Illinois College of Medicine in Chicago. He was class president and graduated as a James Scholar. He currently is completing training in ophthalmology at Northwestern University in Chicago.

Index

Notes

Notes

Notes

13, 52, 54, 55, 181.